This book is dedicated to Fu Hsi, who deserves all credit for the creation of the I Ching, to King Wen, who renamed all the kua during his year in prison in 1143 B.C., and to his son Tan, known as the Duke of Chou, who added the meaning and text to all 384 lines, completed in 1109 B.C.

This book is also dedicated to all those seekers of wisdom who came after them and who have kept the wisdom alive and intact for thousands of years—and to those of you who will partake of this great wisdom and carry it forward through the ages.

FU HSI RISING FROM THE MOUNTAIN
DESIGNING THE EIGHT GREAT SIGNS.

the i·ching

THE BOOK OF ANSWERS

THE

i·ching

The Book *of* Answers

NEW REVISED EDITION

INTERPRETED BY
WU WEI

POWER PRESS
LOS ANGELES, CALIFORNIA

Library of Congress Control Number: 2005900613

ISBN: 0-943015-41-3

New Revised Edition 10 9 8 7 6 5 4 3

For information, address:

       Power Press
       6428 Meadows Court
       Malibu, California, 90265
       Telephone: 310/392-9393
       E-mail: wuwei@power-press.com
       Website: www.power-press.com

Cover design: Roger Gefvert
Interior design and production: Robert S. Tinnon Design
All interior art by Wu Wei

The symbol on the title page is the Chinese word picture for change. It was painted with five quick slashes of Wu Wei's ink brush.

Contents

PART FIVE: THE KUA   73

Acknowledgments

I take this moment to acknowledge and thank my son, Pax, for the enormous contribution he made to this newly revised edition of the *I Ching*. Pax's understanding of the universal principles that lie beneath the inner workings of the I Ching, and his personal philosophy, which is so reminiscent of the writing of Lao Tzu and Confucius, were powerfully infused into this present work. He has done thousands of readings for himself and for others, and he knows from experience that good fortune and misfortune hang in the balance on each word of the text. He and I spent many an hour wrestling to find exactly the right words and phrases that would convey the meaning of the ancient texts so you could be correctly guided in your search for wisdom and good fortune. We both rely on the use of the I Ching in making important decisions, and the guidance we write for you is the guidance upon which we ourselves rely.

I also want to thank Monica Faulkner for her fine editing skills, for the contribution of her insightful suggestions, and for her sensitivity to the work that have added so greatly to this new edition.

I also want to thank Roger Gefvert for his enlightened cover design, which set the standard for the beauty of the book and reflects so well the look and feel of the timeless quality of the I Ching itself.

And I want to thank Robert Tinnon for his inspired interior design and layout, which correspond so well to the cover and to the clarity and spirituality of the I Ching.

PUBLISHER'S NOTE

I am pleased and honored to present this newly revised edition of Wu Wei's *The I Ching: The Book of Answers*. In my humble opinion, Wu Wei's *The I Ching: The Book of Answers* provides far greater accuracy and clarity in obtaining answers than any other version because it was written solely for that purpose. When asking questions of the I Ching, we expect clear, well-defined answers, and, most importantly, answers that are not ambiguous, meaning that we are not presented with the possibility of several different courses of action. Wu Wei's revision masterfully accomplishes that goal. Although the language is plain and simple, it still retains the spirit and wisdom of the ancient text while remaining perfectly true to its meaning. It is my hope that this newly revised edition will render the I Ching more accessible to more readers.

MORGAN LEWIS

AUTHOR'S APOLOGY

With regard to my work, I prostrate myself before Fu Hsi and the other great sages who deserve all credit for the conception and formation of the I Ching, and I humbly apologize for my audacity even to approach their most honored and revered work, much less to apply my feeble mind to the task of interpreting what they have written. That I do so is only because of my love for their work and because I wish to provide a version of the I Ching that will give greater clarity in answering those questions that are vital to our well-being. Please accept my minor labors in that spirit.

Your insignificant and lowly servant,

IT IS SAID OF THE

ANCIENT BOOK OF WISDOM:

Neither far nor near,
neither dark nor deep
exist for it.

Wu Wei's comment:
Our questions are endless, but so are the answers: answers that provide perfect solutions for our most vital and difficult questions. That is because the Universe, the totally alive, completely aware Universe of which we are an inseparable part, wants us to have this profound knowledge that is so essential for our well-being. Nothing is hidden from it; it sees into the heart of everything.

the i·ching
THE BOOK OF ANSWERS

part one

INTRODUCTION

 *Introduction*

If you knew which of your actions would bring you good fortune and which misfortune, which actions would lead to your success and which to failure, would that knowledge not be better than gold and diamonds? Would it not allow you to achieve any goal? Have anything you desired? If you could transcend the barriers of time to look into the future, into the past, if you could see the road that led to happiness, the road to despair, would you not consider yourself fortunate indeed?

When you become adept in the use of the I Ching, you will be able to do all those things and more. Open your mind to the words on the following pages; allow yourself the freedom, the luxury, to believe that all of the above is possible.

We are part of the Universe—each one of us—as much a part as are the galaxies that whirl through space and, here on our little planet, as much a part as are the trees, the mountains, and the sky. We are no less a part of the Universe than anything else is or was or ever can be. We are an integral part, made of the same stuff as the rest of the Universe: Universal energy. All *is* one.

The Universe is alive, conscious, and aware—acutely aware of each of us. And how could it be otherwise since we are it? The Universe experiences itself through us . . . and through the breeze blowing through the trees, the snail crawling on the ground, the lightning that strikes the mountain top, and the galaxies that whirl through space.

The Universe wants to continue. How do we know? Because it does . . . that means that all the laws of the Universe are in favor of continuation. If there was even one law that favored discontinuation, surely destruction would have come to pass during the billions of years since it all began. But, it has not come to pass. That also means that everything that happens is perfect—must be perfect—that the Universe will not tolerate anything less. If it could, it would be in danger of its own destruction because one imperfect event could lead to two, to three, to four, and so on, leading to destruction. It never allows even the first imperfect event to occur. That means that since we are the Universe, a part of it, everything that happens benefits us. It may hurt us or take something away from us, but it always benefits us. If we act on the basis of that, Universal law will bring peace to our souls and joy to our hearts.

Everything that happens, happens within time. We like to think that time stretches illimitably forward into the future and illimitably back into the past while we exist on a hairline of time that separates the future from the past, the hairline we call "Now." Quite the reverse is true; all there is and was and ever will be is an endless "Now," within which change occurs.

Within that endless "Now," we are eternal, all of us, as is everything else, simply changing—endlessly.

Because we are the Universe, a part of it, and because time is a living, breathing entity that contains conscious-ness—may indeed *be* the consciousness of the Universe, per-meating everything, including ourselves—we can know everything the Universe knows; all we need is a key to un-lock that fount of sublime wisdom and complete informa-tion. That we each have a key is unquestionable; every time a new idea seems to arise spontaneously within us we have used our key. Egotistically, we like to think that we created the idea, but actually what we did was no less noteworthy: we channeled the idea from the source; we used our key. We know that the Universe wants us to have that knowledge be-cause we have been provided with the key.

That the key exists within each of us is the premise of all divination. Divination surmises that there is a part of us that is at one with everything, including time, and therefore knows what everything knows. The English root word of divination is *divine*. The Latin root word is *divinus*, mean-ing a deity, and also, to foretell!

For us to be able to draw from the fount of Universal wisdom, we must have a means to do so. Some people draw from the fount with prayer; some by meditating; some by being quiet and focusing their attention on the subject under question, or no question at all; some by talking with psychics or astrologers; others by manipulating objects such as coins, tarot cards, ruins, yarrow stalks, or any of a number of related objects; still others by interpreting dreams.

All of the systems work perfectly, up to the limits of the systems and the capability of the questioner or interpreter. If, for instance, you ask a question and flip a coin to get an answer, you are limited to a yes or no answer. If you ask a question and select from a deck of cards with several sentences of guidance printed on it, you can obtain counsel beyond yes or no. The more sophisticated the system, the more complete and detailed will be the answer.

If you and I decided to formulate a system to obtain answers to questions, we would put into that system as many answers as there are questions. That may sound difficult, even impossible, but one answer can be sufficient for many questions. For instance, all questions regarding the taking of action can be generally satisfied with three answers: to take action, to take no action, or to delay taking action. Fortunately, we do not have to create a system of answers: the I Ching masterfully fills that need. Once the answers have been formulated, all that remains is to devise a method for determining which answer applies to which question. Because we are searching for cosmic answers, we must prevent ourselves from intellectually tampering with how we obtain the results, a method that will permit only the spiritual portion of ourselves—that portion that is at one with All-That-Is—to participate; the yarrow stalk method perfectly accomplishes that end.

When we close our eyes and grasp a number of yarrow stalks from a bunch of forty-nine stalks, when we select a card from a deck whose faces we cannot see, when we choose a stone from a pile of inscribed stones whose faces we cannot see, or in following similar practices, we exceed our intellectual ability to determine the outcome because we cannot know how many stalks were grasped, or which card was chosen until its face is seen, or which stone was chosen from the pile until the inscription on its face can be read. All such methods of choosing rely completely on the intuitive ability of the questioner, on his ability to draw upon his spiritual source that knows everything. In the words of Lao Tzu, ". . . to feel beyond touch . . . to hear beyond sound . . . to see beyond shape, and . . . to tell beyond words."

When all our answers have been developed and our method of selecting answers has been determined, we can proceed confidently to ask questions because there is a part within each of us that knows the answers to all our questions and that will guide us in choosing the correct answer.

Fu Hsi (pronounced *foo shee*), the great Chinese sage to whom the I Ching system is attributed, constructed his answers in the form of sixty-four six-line figures the Chinese

call *kua*, each line stacked one above the other, either solid
(—), or broken (- -). Each of the kua is formed by combining two of eight basic trigrams, which are three-line figures such as this: (≡ ≡). The two trigrams that form the kua
(≣)are called *primary trigrams.* There are two other trigrams in the kua called *nuclear trigrams,* which will later
be described in detail.

Before the lines exist, there are six empty spaces. The lines
fill those spaces and move within them. Following the law of
eternal change, the lines are always in motion, always moving
upward. As a new line enters from the bottom, it pushes the five
lines above it upward, thereby displacing the line at the top. The
movement always follows the rhythm of the Universal heartbeat, always mirroring the Universe itself. Taken together, the
kua and their lines represent every conceivable condition in
Heaven and on Earth with all their states of change.

Each of the sixty-four kua can change into one another
through the movement of one or more of the six lines that
form the kua. There are 4,096 possible combinations (64
× 64), which represent every possible condition in Heaven
and on Earth.

The kua and trigrams are both called *kua* (pronounced
"gwa," with the "a" sounded as in father), which means *symbol.* To avoid confusion, but to retain the flavor of the ancient text as much as possible, the six-line figures will be
referred to as *kua* and the three-line figures as *trigrams.*

Each of the sixty-four kua, with their combined total of 384 lines, represents a situation or condition. Each situation or condition contains the six stages of its own evolution: 1. *about to come into being*, 2. *beginning*, 3. *expanding*, 4. *approaching maximum potential*, 5. *peaking*, and 6. *passing its peak* and *turning toward its opposite condition*. By taking the appropriate action, we can turn any condition into any other condition. (See my *A Tale of the I Ching*, Power Press)

The kua not only represent every conceivable situation and condition possible, but also include all their states of change. Fu Hsi's method for selecting the appropriate kua is unique: the manipulation of fifty yarrow stalks, one being laid aside as an observer stalk, the rest being divided and re-divided eighteen times.

Does the system work? Yes. Does it work perfectly? Yes. Every time? Yes. Will it work perfectly for you? Yes, if you seek the truth with reverence and sincerity. Why? Because you are a Divine Being in an eternal Universe of which you are an inseparable part, which is an inexhaustible wellspring of cosmic information from which you may freely draw. Can you draw from it correct answers to hurt another? No. Can you draw from it correct answers to gain an unfair advantage? No. Can you draw from it correct answers if you will misuse the information? No. All guidance given in the I Ching is virtuous, beneficial, and given with the intent of guiding you along the highest possible path for your greatest possible good and the greatest possible good of everyone and everything else. You will not be assisted by your higher self to commit acts harmful to yourself or to another.

Will frivolous questions be answered? Yes, frivolously. Will questions that imply doubt in the source of the answers be answered? Yes, but only in a way that will confirm the doubt in your mind; you cannot run a test on your own divinity.

How can you be certain the answers are correct? After you have received an answer to a vitally important question and feel everything within you resonating with the truth, wisdom, and guidance contained in the answer—a resonance so pure and sweet that it brings joy to your heart, and sometimes tears to your eyes—you will, at that moment, be certain that the question was perfectly answered, divinely answered. At those moments you can experience your oneness with All-That-Is. Once having had the experience, you will never again wonder who it is or what it is that is answering your questions or whether the answers are correct.

In the I Ching you can read that teaching is a holy task, to be withheld from no one. You can derive from that statement that the answers provided in the I Ching are given in the form of guidance, of teaching, which will not be withheld from you. Not only will you be provided with answers to questions, but you will also be given counsel concerning the best way to proceed to obtain a particular result. Additionally, under certain circumstances, you will be told what condition will replace the current condition. For the divine within you, time is not a barrier nor is distance.

Fu Hsi perceived the laws of the Universe and set them forth so that we could be guided, so that we could be free, so that we would no longer be subject to the tyranny of events, and so that each of us could be in charge of our own fate. He created the sixty-four kua so that we could know the operation of the Universe and so that within the Universe each of us could find our place. He spoke in terms of "good fortune" and "misfortune." Good fortune brings you good friends, security, food, clothing, good health, shelter, opportunity, wealth, a good mate, and windfall good luck. Misfortune takes any or all of those same things away from you.

Fu Hsi spoke of the paths of life, calling the path that leads to good fortune "the way of the superior person" and the path that leads to misfortune "the way of the inferior person." The path of the superior person is the path of abundant life. That path is narrow in one sense and broad in another. It is narrow in that it does not stray into areas of dishonesty, selfishness, debauchery, harmful intentions, and unclean living. It is broad in the sense that it encompasses everything else that is in keeping with virtue, honor, clean living, good intentions, and integrity. The path of abundant life is filled with love, happiness, abundance, and success. We know when we are on that path when we are experiencing joy, happiness, and great good fortune. The path that leads away from abundant life can be discerned by our experiencing pain, unhappiness, and great misfortune. That path has many pitfalls, but they are of our own creation, even though it seems as if forces outside of us are creating them. The need for punishment arises when we have deviated from the path of abundant life and need the pitfalls to direct us back onto the correct path. Fu Hsi spoke in terms of *good* and *evil*. In modern times we rarely hear these terms used, but for this present work they have been preserved because they impart a sense of who Fu Hsi was, and they retain the flavor of the ancient texts.

We live in a perfect Universe in which only perfect events can unfold: the Universe will not tolerate anything else; if it could or would, it would be in danger of permitting its own destruction. That information must live in your consciousness if you are to lead a happy life, free of needless worry and frustration.

One of the great truths that can be gained from a study of the I Ching is that the Universe is powerfully inclined in our favor; there is more of the good force than the seeming bad force—that is why and how the Universe persists— and that is why you can always triumph over any evil force if you are good enough. The way to do that is not to combat evil directly—thereby becoming an instrument of evil—but to make energetic progress in the good, following Fu Hsi's path of the superior person that leads unerringly to the greatest states that humans can desire.

Remember that the greatest honor one can have is to be part of the Universe. You have been selected to have that honor. Remember also that the greatest spiritual experience one can have is simply to be who you are at any moment, including this one.

My fellow traveler, I wish you well. May you mount to the skies of success as though on the wings of six dragons!

Your humble and insignificant servant,

part two
THE BEGINNING

A Brief History of the I Ching

Thousands of years ago, before the dawn of written history, legend has it that there lived a great Chinese sage known as Fu Hsi. He is reputed to be the man who first united all of China and became its first emperor. He is also credited with leading the Chinese people from the age of hunting and fishing into the age of agriculture. As you can imagine, that was a long, long time ago—six thousand years at the earliest, and, more likely, ten thousand.

A man of incredibly vast intellect, and a man whose psychic channels were obviously open, Fu Hsi drew forth from the Universal mind, over a period of time and in stages, a perfect mathematical model of itself, complete with all its conditions and elements of change—the sixty-four six-line symbols that the Chinese call the kua and that make up the I Ching. (The complete story of how I believe Fu Hsi formulated his model can be found in my book *A Tale of the I Ching*, Power Press.)

To form the sixty-four kua, Fu Hsi, it is said, surveyed the vast diversities and movements under Heaven, saw the ways that the movements met and became interrelated, and saw how their courses were governed by eternal laws. He thought through the order of the outer world to its end and explored his own nature to its deepest core. He perceived the beginning of all things that lay unmoving in the "beyond" in the form of ideas that had yet to manifest themselves. He put himself in accord with those ideas and, in so doing, arrived at an understanding of fate. It is also quite possible that he simply received that information in the form of a communication from the Universe, as a waking dream, or a sleeping dream, or a vision in meditation, or in a moment of clarity while walking through the forest, as we ourselves do when we perceive a new idea. When the Universe wants to communicate with us, it uses whatever means are at hand.

Writing did not exist at the time of Fu Hsi, so his teachings were handed down in the oral tradition, with one generation faithfully teaching another for thousands of years. It was the most valuable information on the planet, and, as such, it was treasured and passed on. In the opinion of this humble author, it still remains the most valuable information on the planet.

When writing came to China, five thousand years ago, around the year 3000 B.C., the I Ching readings were the first information to be recorded. Two thousand more years passed, during which time the I Ching and its teachings flourished.

In the twelfth century B.C., the tyrant Chou Shin ruled. He was to be the last emperor of the Yin Dynasty. He was a cruel and heartless man who tortured people to please his equally cruel and sadistic concubine. So cruel was he that all of China lived in fear of him.

At the same time, there also lived a man named Wen, a direct descendant of Fu Hsi and a learned I Ching scholar of rare insight who governed a small province in a remote area of western China. Wen governed his people according to I Ching principles and was therefore as much loved and respected by the people as Chou Shin was hated and feared. The people urged Wen to gather an army and overthrow the tyrant. They assured him that all the people would follow him willingly. But he replied that, because he was truly a law-abiding citizen, he could not in good conscience take action against the emperor.

Unfortunately for Wen, but fortunately for the rest of us, Chou Shin heard the rumors that Wen was being asked to lead an uprising and had him arrested and put into prison. Wen was allowed to live, seemingly because of his great popularity, but actually so he could make his wonderful contribution to the refinement of the I Ching.

During the year 1143 B.C., the year that Wen spent in confinement and in fear for his life, he used the I Ching's great wisdom and its divinatory powers to keep himself alive. In Wen's time, there were two versions of the I Ching, the Lien Sah and the Gai Tsen.

Neither one offered any guidance other than the six lines of the kua. During his imprisonment, Wen provided the names of the kua and described the condition or situation that each of them portrayed—what we know of today as the opening paragraphs of the kua. He also changed the order of the kua established by Fu Hsi to the order currently in use in every version of the I Ching. (The order of the kua does not in any way affect the readings.)

In 1122 B.C., Wen's oldest son, Wu, publicly denounced Chou Shin to turn public opinion against him, gathered an army, overthrew the tyrant, and became emperor. To honor his father, who had passed away, Wu posthumously bestowed upon him the title of "king," and Wen was forever after known as King Wen, even though he never ruled as king. Wu died a few years after becoming king and left his thirteen-year-old son as heir to the throne. The inexperienced youngster obviously was incapable of ruling, so Wu's brother, Tan, known as the Duke of Chou, ruled in his stead. Wen had instructed Tan in the teachings of the I Ching, and it was Tan who, during his reign as acting king, interpreted the meanings of the individual lines and added the text to each line as we know it today. The I Ching was then considered complete. The year was 1109 B.C.

In A.D. 1700, the Khang Hsi editors prepared the current version of the I Ching along with commentaries from more than three hundred different scholars who had written them over a period of three thousand years. The document was completed in A.D. 1715 and is the version that everyone translates into today's version of the I Ching.

So profound was the wisdom that King Wen and his sons derived from study of the I Ching that they were able to found a dynasty so strong that it lasted for nine hundred years, the longest in the history of China. As you might imagine, they also used the I Ching to gain insight and to receive Universal guidance in making decisions.

Several hundred years later, in the fifth century B.C., the great sage and scholar Confucius came on the world scene. It is said that he was a homely man, almost seven feet tall and with a hump on his back. He distinguished himself by studying court etiquette, and so thoroughly did he learn it that the emperor sought him out for guidance. He became famous not only for his knowledge of court etiquette but also for his great common sense. At the age of fifty, Confucius began the study of the I Ching, and when he was past the age of seventy, he humorously commented, "If some years were added to my life, I would give fifty to the study of the I Ching, and might then escape from falling into great errors."

Confucius wrote many commentaries regarding the I Ching. Most of these are reproduced in other volumes of the *I Ching*, notably the wonderful Wilhelm/Baynes translation published by Princeton University Press (Bollingen Series XIX). Should you become so engaged with the I Ching that you wish to go beyond using it as an oracle and to begin studying it, you will surely want to consult that most thorough work.

About the I Ching

As used in the title, "I" means "change," and "Ching" means "book." Therefore, it is "The Book of Change," or, as it has come to be known, "The Book of Changes." In this present work I have called it the "Book of Answers" so that those new to the great book will understand its purpose more clearly.

In the known Universe, everything is constantly changing. For any book of wisdom or divination to correctly portray the conditions of the Universe and to be useful, it must reflect the process of change. The I Ching masterfully accomplishes that with its changing lines that create a new kua. Each of the trigrams and kua has a Chinese name that expresses its meaning. Because the Chinese language developed as a language that used characters rather than an alphabet, many Chinese words share the same name and sound but have different meanings and are written using different characters. Usually, listeners can understand which word is meant from the context, and slight variations in pronunciation also help.

The same holds for the kua. Several appear to have
the same name, but they actually have different meanings. For example, Kua 8 and 22 are both called "Pi,"
but Kua 8 means "Joining, Supporting, Uniting" and
Kua 22 means "Outer Refinement." Also, of course,
the arrangement of lines in the two kua differs.

To make it as easy as possible for you to understand and use the kua, Part 5, "The Kua," lists each kua with
the number that King Wen assigned to it, its Chinese name,
and its English meaning or meanings. Because the kua are
concepts, sometimes two or three English words or phrases
are appropriate.

Also, there is a Pronunciation and Spelling Guide starting on page 381 for the sixty-four kua and the eight trigrams.
Over time, scholars have developed several systems for
spelling out Chinese words and sounds in English. Some
books about the I Ching use the traditional Wade-Giles
spelling, and out of respect for tradition, that is the one I
use. Other writers have begun using a more recent spelling
system called *Pinyin*. The Pronunciation and Spelling Guide
lists all the kua and trigrams according to both spellings. You
may find it helpful if you decide to make a deeper study of
the I Ching.

part three

THE MEANING OF THE KUA, THE TRIGRAMS, AND THE LINES

The Meaning of the Kua

The meaning of each kua is generally derived from the attributes of the two trigrams from which it is formed. For example, the meaning of Kua 11, T'ai, is "Peaceful Prosperity and Harmony." It is comprised of the trigram of Ch'ien (☰), which represents Heaven, and K'un (☷), which represents Earth. Earth is over Heaven. The tendency of Earth is to sink, and the tendency of Heaven is to rise. Therefore, the two come together, bringing about a time of "Heaven on Earth" or "Peaceful Prosperity and Harmony."

KUA 11

Sometimes the names and the meanings of the kua are taken from what the six-line figure looks like. For example, Kua 50, Ting, "The Cauldron," resembles a big pot.

KUA 50

The broken bottom line represents the legs; the next three solid lines represent the belly of the pot; the next broken line, the rings or handles by which it is carried; and the top solid line, the lid.

Some of the kua take their meanings from the action of the lines, as in Kua 43, Kuai, which means "Overthrow of the Dark Force." The five lower solid lines represent a strong and virtuous person, usually you, who is moving upward to overthrow the top line, which, being broken, represents a dark force or an evil person or people.

KUA 43

The next section lists the eight primary trigrams, along with the subjects and the attributes or qualities that the trigrams represent. The attributes or qualities do not necessarily apply to the subjects. Two examples will show what I mean.

The trigram "Ch'ien" represents "Heaven," "the father," and "males," and its attributes are "creative," "strong," and "virtuous." That does not mean that all males are creative, strong, and virtuous. Also, in Kua 43, Kuai, mentioned earlier, which represents "Overthrow of the Dark Force," the person represented by the broken top line of the kua could be either an evil man or an evil woman, depending on the circumstances surrounding your question.

THE EIGHT TRIGRAMS AND THEIR ATTRIBUTES

CH'IEN
THE CREATIVE

Heaven, God, strong, male, light-giving, virtuous, good, direct, aggressive, forceful, rigid, unyielding. It is the element that stimulates K'un to bring forth All-That-Is. It is the original, ultimate source. (The motion of the trigram is upward.)

K'UN
THE RECEPTIVE

Earth, mother, female yielding, receptive, gentle, devoted, hollow. It is the element through which Ch'ien brings into being All-That-Is. K'un is the Receptive in that it purely receives, without resistance, all that Ch'ien commands. (The motion of the trigram is downward.)

NOTE: Neither Ch'ien nor K'un is greater than the other, nor are they opposites. They work together to bring into being All-That-Is. Neither one can bring things into a state of being without the help of the other.

CHÊN
AROUSING

Thunder, the force that excites to action, the oldest son, development, forceful. (The motion of the trigram is upward.)

SUN
WIND, WOOD

Penetrating, oldest daughter, gentle, adaptive, a tree, influence. (The motion of the trigram is downward.)

K'AN
WATER, THE ABYSS

Danger, rain, middle son, blood, fear, moon, dark, winter, work, a pit, as in a deep hole. (The motion of the trigram is downward.)

LI
FIRE

Light, reason, clarity, middle daughter, flying bird, flame, cow, weapons. It clings to that which nourishes it as flame to wood or grass to earth. (The motion of the trigram is upward.)

KÊN
MOUNTAIN

Stopping, heavy, youngest son, unmoving, calm, a gate or a door, pausing, inner reserve. (The motion of the trigram is downward.)

T'UI
MARSH, LAKE

Joyous, reservoir, marsh, youngest daughter, gaiety, mouth, magician, pleasure, to break in pieces or to break apart. (The motion of the trigram is upward.)

INNER AND
OUTER TRIGRAMS

The upper trigram is said to be the outer trigram; the lower trigram is said to be the inner trigram.

An example of how the inner and outer trigrams give meaning to the kua can be seen in Kua 15, Ch'ien, "Modesty." The lower trigram is Kên (☶), which means mountain, and the upper trigram is K'un, or Earth (☷). The meaning is therefore a mountain hidden within the Earth, or the image of modesty.

KUA 15

Another example is Kua 29, K'an, "Danger." When the lower trigram is the trigram K'an, the danger exists within the situation. When upper trigram is the trigram K'an, the danger is coming from outside the situation.

KUA 29

NUCLEAR
TRIGRAMS

Each kua contains two "nuclear" trigrams. They are called nuclear because they are made up of Lines 2, 3, 4, and 5, or the middle four lines of the kua.

The nuclear trigrams influence the meaning of the individual lines more than they influence the overall meaning of the kua.

The lower nuclear trigram is formed from Lines 2, 3, and 4. The upper nuclear trigram is formed from Lines 3, 4, and 5. Lines 1 and 6 are not affected by the nuclear trigrams because they are not part of either of them.

Line 2 of the kua is part of two trigrams: the lower primary trigram, of which it is the center line, and the lower nuclear trigram, of which it is the bottom line.

Line 3 is part of three trigrams: the lower primary trigram, of which it is the top line, the lower nuclear trigram, of which it is the center line, and the upper nuclear trigram, of which it is the bottom line.

Line 4 is also part of three trigrams: the lower nuclear trigram, of which it is the top line, the upper nuclear trigram, of which it is the middle line, and the upper primary trigram, of which it is the bottom line.

Like Line 2, Line 5 is part of two trigrams: the upper nuclear trigram, of which it forms the top line, and the upper primary trigram, of which it forms the middle line.

If a particular line has meaning for you, that is, if it is a moving line and the line is either number 2, 3, 4, or 5, the line will be subtly influenced by the nuclear trigram or trigrams of which it is a part. What the specific influence is will be determined by the nature of the nuclear trigram itself. For instance, if the nuclear trigram is danger, there will be a hint of danger in the situation, and the counsel of the moving line may add a word of caution.

THE LINES

CHARACTERISTICS

Generally speaking, the characteristics of the solid and the broken lines are as follows:

SOLID	BROKEN
Strong	Weak
Virtuous	Evil
Light-giving	Dark
Aggressive	Gentle

The characteristics of either kind of line can be modified by the meaning of the kua, but such modifications will always be stated in the kua.

CORRECTNESS

Before a kua is formed, there are six empty places that the lines will fill. Three of the places require strong lines, meaning solid lines, and three require weak lines, meaning broken lines. Places 1, 3, and 5 are strong and require strong, solid lines. Those lines are then considered correct because they are strong lines in strong places.

Places 2, 4, and 6 require weak, broken lines. Those lines are then considered correct because they are weak lines in weak places. When a weak line is in a place that calls for a strong line, it is generally unequal to the task at hand. When a strong line is in a place that calls for a weak line, it is generally too aggressive for the task at hand.

Keep in mind that those are general rules and can be modified according to a particular situation or condition, but any such special conditions will always be stated in the discussion of each kua.

CORRESPONDENCE

Each of the lines corresponds to one other line. Line 1, the bottom line of the lower trigram, corresponds to Line 4, the bottom line of the upper trigram. Similarly, Line 2, the middle line of the lower trigram, corresponds to Line 5, the middle line of the upper trigram. Line 3, the top line of the lower trigram, corresponds to Line 6, the top line of the upper trigram.

When corresponding lines are the same, either both broken or both solid, they generally oppose and repel each other, the way two magnets will repel each other if you try to place their positive ends together. When corresponding lines are different, they are helpful to each other. For instance, when a strong ruler (represented by a solid Line 5), has a compliant subordinate, official, or minister (represented by a broken Line 2), there is no conflict, and the subordinate carries out the ruler's orders.

If the ruler is weak (represented by a broken Line 5) and the subordinate strong (represented by a solid Line 2), the ruler can still rely on the trustworthy subordinate to carry out orders. If both the ruler and the subordinate are strong, the chances are that the subordinate will be headstrong, argumentative, and insubordinate—not a good condition. If both the ruler and the subordinate are weak, they will not be able to make progress. Remember that this is a general rule and can be overridden by a particular situation or condition as detailed in the discussion of each kua.

CONDITION

The Bottom Line indicates the onset of the condition depicted in the kua. It has just barely begun to manifest itself.

Line 2 shows the condition beginning to grow stronger, but because of the favorableness of the line, being in the center of the lower trigram, the condition is usually under control.

Line 3 is at the top of the lower trigram, so the condition has grown stronger and is usually unstable because Line 3 is about to leave the lower trigram for the upper, which is nearly always somewhat dangerous.

Line 4 shows that the condition is approaching its maximum potential. Therefore, depending on whether the condition bodes good or evil, one must be cautious. Additional caution is required because Line 4 is next to Line 5, which is generally the ruler. Being close to a ruler can be very good, but it can also be very dangerous. If the situation warrants it, the kua will state which condition prevails.

Line 5 shows the condition having reached its maximum potential. Any movement beyond that point will cause the condition to exceed its maximum potential and turn it toward its opposite: fullness to emptiness, increase to decrease, abundance to want.

The Top Line usually shows the condition depicted in the kua having exceeded its maximum potential and consequently turning toward its opposite condition.

POSITION

The Bottom Line can represent a newcomer, someone just about to join a group, or a subordinate in the lowest position. That person will generally lack any title or influence.

Line 2 occupies the center of the lower trigram and indicates that the person it represents is in a position of leadership but subordinate to Line 5, which is the place of the prince or king. The person has some authority, and in an organization may have a title. In the army, such a person would be a lieutenant, a sergeant, or possibly a general. Being in the center of the lower trigram, this person will have some influence with peers or associates and is connected to the leader, Line 5.

Line 3 is the top line of the lower trigram and represents a person who is rising in the ranks. This person has attained some stature and is about to advance to the upper trigram, a somewhat dangerous move. The danger in the move is due to the necessity of leaving the position in the lower trigram and "jumping" into the upper trigram. The time between jumping and landing is dangerous.

Line 4 is next to the ruler, which can be fortunate or dangerous, or both, depending on the circumstances. The person who is the subject of Line 4 is considered to be the ruler's minister, an able general, a partner, or a strong vice president. This person is usually in a position of trust. It is almost always beneficial for the ruler and the minister to be represented by lines of a different character, meaning broken and solid lines, for that means that they will not be in conflict, as was previously discussed in the section on "Correspondence."

Line 5 occupies the center of the upper trigram, which is generally the position of the ruler. This line usually controls the kua. It is almost always beneficial if this line is the opposite of Lines 2 and 4 so that conflict is avoided. When it is beneficial for the lines not to be opposite, the kua will so state.

In ancient times, the Top Line represented a great sage who had left the affairs of the world behind but could be called upon in any great emergency. Today, it could represent a retired person who has served his or her country, organization, or family well and has retreated from worldly affairs but still has influence.

TIME

Each of the lines represents a time earlier or later in the kua according to its position. The Bottom Line represents the earliest time and the Top Line the latest time. Only the four middle lines represent the time that is active within the situation. Line 1 represents the time just before the active time. Line 6 represents the time just after the active time.

However, in the case of moving lines, the first moving line usually depicts the immediate action to take or avoid, even if it is in Line 2 or higher. Higher moving lines depict later times in the situation. That is why two lines can contradict each other and still be valid. It just means that the first moving line refers to now or to soon after now, and the other line or lines refer to later.

HOLDING TOGETHER

Lines next to each other hold together if they are different and do not hold together if they are the same. The most important of these relationships is that of the Lines 4 and 5, the ruler and subordinate, and, as discussed previously in the section on "Correspondence," the best condition for those two lines is when the ruler is strong and the subordinate weak. The line on top is said to "rest" on the line below, and the line below is said to "receive" from the line above.

If a broken line rests on a solid line below, the broken line is well supported. If a solid line rests on a broken line, the support is weak. If a broken line receives from a solid line above, the broken line is benefited because of the strength of the solid line.

If a solid line receives from a broken line, the solid line is not usually benefited because of the weakness of the broken line. This is a general rule, and any departures will be stated in the kua.

HEAVEN, EARTH, AND MAN

Starting at the bottom of the kua, the first two lines represent Earth, the middle two lines represent Man, and the top two lines represent Heaven. Man in the middle is the entity through which Heaven and Earth interact.

DOUBLED TRIGRAMS

There are eight instances when a kua is made up of the same trigram doubled. In these instances, the kua's name is that

of the doubled trigram, and its meaning is in-
tensified. You are to pay extra heed to the guidance given or the situation depicted. For instance,
in Kua 29, K'an, "Danger," which depicts the element of danger, the danger is extreme and comes both from
an inner and outer source.

KUA 29

These are the eight doubled trigrams:

KUA 1, CH'IEN

KUA 2, K'UN

KUA 29, K'AN

KUA 30, LI

KUA 51, CHÊN

KUA 52, KÊN

KUA 57, SUN

KUA 58, TUI

THE PROCESS OF DIVINATION

Following are the basic steps for consulting I Ching. They are described in complete detail in Part 4, page 61.

1. You write down a carefully formulated question. The next section, "Phrasing Questions," page 44, describes how to develop questions that will give you the most appropriate counsel.
2. You hold the question in mind and divide the yarrow stalks as described in "The Yarrow Stalk Method" on page 61.
3. The numbers derived from the manipulation of the yarrow stalks lead to the formation of a first

line, then a second and so on, until the six lines of
the kua are formed.

4. A key on page 403 shows the number of the kua
   and the page on which it is found.

5. The opening paragraphs of the kua are read. If you
   are new or relatively new to the I Ching, read all six
   lines of the kua to gain a better understanding of
   its overall meaning.

6. If you obtain lines with either the number 6 or the
   number 9, called "moving lines," these are taken
   into consideration in the answer to the question.
   The other lines are disregarded.

7. The lines obtained with either a 6 or a 9, if any,
   have so much energy that they are changed to their
   opposite: broken to solid, solid to broken. Those
   transformed lines, along with the other lines that
   were not transformed, form a new kua that will
   provide additional guidance or indicate what the
   future holds.

8. Consult the chart on page 403 again to find the
   number and page number for the new kua, which
   is read only for its meaning.

   None of the lines of the new kua are to be taken
   into consideration in the answer, but you may
   read them to help you perceive the overall meaning
   of the kua.

PHRASING QUESTIONS

You can ask "yes" or "no" questions, but there are better ways to phrase your questions. The I Ching does not contain "yes" or "no" answers. But if you ask a question that requires a "yes" or "no" answer such as, "Should I marry now?" and you receive as an answer the kua of "Strong Restraint," your answer would be clear. A more meaningful answer can be obtained if you ask, "What can I expect if I marry now?" Depending on your answer, you might then want to ask, "What can I expect if I marry later?" Intelligent, well-thought-out questions will be the most rewarding.

It is essential that you write out your questions. It will also be helpful if you write a little about the conditions surrounding your question. Here is an example of what you might write:

> The house we are renting is for sale. We would like to buy the house, but it would strain our resources to the limit. My husband has just taken a new job, and there is a small possibility that he will be transferred, which would necessitate our reselling the house. What can we expect if we buy the house now?

By writing out the conditions surrounding your question, you will find that it is easier to formulate it. Initially, you would probably think to ask whether you should buy the house now.

Writing out the conditions surrounding your question makes it clear that you should also ask what you and your husband can expect if he is transferred, and if you do not want him to be transferred, he might ask, "What can I do to avoid being transferred?"

Using the I Ching gives you the awareness that you do not have to be pushed around willy-nilly by fate, and that by taking the appropriate action you can determine your own fate. For example, asking whether you will make a lot of money this year indicates that you are not in control. A better question is, "What can I do to increase my earnings this year?" Asking what action you should take to create a particular result is a always a good question and demonstrates your awareness that you can control your affairs.

Always write the date, the time, and your location at the top of the page on which you write your question for later reference.

It will also be of great benefit to write the answer to your question on the same page as that upon which you wrote your question.

Keep the pages in a binder or folder so that you can refer to them at a later time. By reviewing your questions and answers occasionally, you will see how events turned out and how the answers applied.

As the years go by, you will be able to look back and see what your concerns were at different times in your life and whether they remained the same or changed. (The *I Ching Workbook*, Power Press, is designed to fill that need.)

AN EXAMPLE

Below, I have asked a question on your behalf for three reasons: first, so you will have an example to follow; second, so you can determine what you could expect in the way of help from using the I Ching; and third, so you can see how the system works. I asked the following question as if I were you.

> February 2, 2005: 7:20 A.M., Riviera Ave. house. I have problems and difficulties and I need help. What can I expect from using the I Ching?

The resulting kua is Kua 59, Huan, "Dissolve, Disintegrate, Dissipate, Unify."

The lines are:

Top Line 6	2, 2, 3 = 7	———
Line 5	3, 3, 3 = 9	——— •
Line 4	3, 2, 3 = 8	— —
Line 3	3, 3, 2 = 8	— —

Line 2	3, 2, 2 = 7	———
Bottom Line	2, 3, 3 = 8	—— ——

Because Line 5 changes, this becomes Kua 4, Mêng (Inexperience).

———
—— ——
—— ——
—— ——
———
—— ——

The text of Kua 59 and the moving line are reproduced below. The five lines that are not to be taken into consideration in the answer are not reproduced. The dot at the end of Line 5 will be explained later.

KUA 59, HUAN, DISSOLVE, DISINTEGRATE, DISSIPATE, UNIFY

This indicates that a dangerous situation exists that you can resolve by identifying the danger and acting to gently dissolve or dispel the dangerous elements. The source of the danger is disunity and a lack of harmony among those who should be unified and cooperating to achieve a common goal. Human elements or traits that can prevent harmony and unity include ego, selfish and divergent self-interests, hostility, anger, greed, hard-heartedness, and even hatred. If there is a lack of enthusiasm and dedication to a common goal, creating and maintaining unity will be difficult.

To obtain help in identifying the heart of the problem and in arriving at ways to dispel the danger, seek the guidance of the Universe in whatever way is appropriate for you, such as again inquiring of the oracle. Speaking with the people involved will help you to learn what is keeping apart those who should be working together. If you make yourself a focal point; provide a common goal around which everyone can rally; and generate enthusiasm; as well as dissolving enmity, anger, hostility, and hatred, you will defeat the dangerous elements that are blocking unity. You will succeed in dissolving even the greatest danger, provided you persevere in searching for its source and in seeking ways to dissolve it. Success is certain.

Line 5: You are strong and in a position of leadership. Despite the dangerous situation at present, in which disunity and conflict prevail, you will be inspired with a great idea that will unite your group. You will communicate it with such enthusiasm that everyone will follow your inspired leadership and thus end the conflict. Remain modest, and do not take credit. Instead, share it with others, and you will remain without blame for your actions.

The kua says that by consulting the I Ching, you will be able to penetrate to the heart of your problems and dissolve them. Line 5 says that you are a strong person and implies that you are in charge of your own destiny (a position of leadership). It states specifically that you will receive inspiring ideas from the I Ching about ways to dissolve your problems. It also offers assurance, saying, "You will succeed in dissolving even the greatest danger, provided you persevere in searching for its source and in seeking ways to dissolve it." A moving line is so called because it is charged with so much energy that it turns into its opposite, a broken line into a solid line and a solid line into a broken line, thereby bringing about the formation of a new kua. Because Line 5 is a moving line, it changes into a broken line, bringing about the formation of a new kua.

The new kua describes what the situation will become, or it supplies additional information. In this case the new kua is 4, Mêng, "Inexperience." It is reproduced here except for the individual lines, which are not taken into consideration:

KUA 4, MÊNG, INEXPERIENCE

When inexperienced persons seek guidance from experienced teachers, they meet with success because it is the teacher's joy and responsibility to teach others. It is important, though, that students have the right attitude toward their teachers. These are some basic guidelines that will help.

First, students must say that they are inexperienced and need guidance.

Second, they should be modest and show the teacher proper respect.

Third, they should never mistrustfully question the teacher more than once about the same question. However, if the answer is truly not understood, additional questions are permissible. Following these simple steps will make the teacher happy to cooperate, and thus the student will continue to learn. This then becomes an amazing time for students because they can learn the great words of wisdom and become expert in their chosen field. That is how teachers lead their students to success.

If you are the teacher and your students continue to doubt your answers or do not show you the respect you deserve, it is wise to abandon your efforts. Some people are not ready to listen to the wise words of a sage. Instead, let them go out in the world, where the Universe will give them what they need for their learning. Over time, they will be molded, shaped, and changed to the point where they will be more willing to listen. There is no saying how long this will take, for it is different with everyone.

This kua offers advice for both students and teachers. You must think about the question you asked and decide which you are. Once you have decided, follow the guidance appropriate for your role.

You are being guided to seek out more information about your quest. You can do this by asking more questions of the I Ching, by researching your subject to gain a greater understanding of it, or by seeking help from a qualified person or mentor. An inexperienced person like yourself will do well to seek guidance from experienced teachers, because that will ultimately lead to your success. It is your task to seek out a teacher, for it is not appropriate for teachers to seek you out. Perseverance in learning brings success, and thoroughness in all that is done shapes character. If you fail to find your teacher or guide, you may also fail to achieve your goal. However, your inexperience, which forces you to find out more, is actually a blessing because your pursuit of knowledge will develop your character and move you further toward your enlightenment. If you proceed in that manner, you will quickly gain understanding and expertise, and you will fly to your goal like a hungry eagle when it has sighted its prey.

As you can see, Mêng states that you are inexperienced and will seek guidance from an experienced teacher. If you doubt the information and continue to ask the same question to see whether you will obtain the same response, the answer you receive will not be intelligible. The kua promises that you will have success and that the information will not be withheld from you. It goes on to say that the success you seek will be obtained by perseverance in seeking guidance and adds that by being thorough you will form character.

The information and guidance provided by Huan and Mêng yield the clear, direct, intelligent, and enlightened answers one expects from a great teacher. Providing answers of this clarity and quality has made the I Ching treasured by billions of people over thousands of years.

A SUGGESTION
FOR THE BEGINNER

If you are new to the use of the I Ching, I suggest that at this point you familiarize yourself with the process of divination by studying the section that follows, Part 4, "Consulting the I Ching," which describes asking questions and the use of the yarrow stalks. When you have gone through the process of asking questions and manipulating the yarrow stalks several times, reread this section.

part four

CONSULTING
THE I CHING

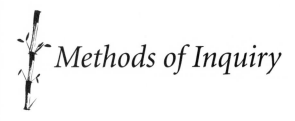

Methods of Inquiry

The ancient sages devised two methods of asking questions: the tortoise shell method and the yarrow stalk method. The answers to the questions were usually carved on bones. Some of those bones have been discovered and represent the earliest writings of the Chinese people.

The tortoise shell method, which entailed heating a tortoise shell until it cracked and its cracks read, is lost to us, but the yarrow stalk method has come down to us intact across thousands of years and will be explained later in detail.

Many people today use a coin method, which is quick and easy. However, because the coins have only three heads and three tails collectively, they lack the mathematical potential to display the unfolding Universe. One of the greatest injuries inflicted on the use of the I Ching was the introduction of the coin method for obtaining answers. It has caused many people to stop using the I Ching because the answers were not quite right all the time. Only yarrow stalks should be used.

THE PRINCIPLE

The yarrow stalk method involves holding forty-nine yarrow stalks in your left hand and grasping a portion of stalks with your right hand. You have no way of knowing how many stalks you have grasped, and so have exceeded the capacity of your rational mind. It is that process that makes it possible for your unconscious to become active. That unconscious part knows exactly how many stalks have been grasped.

Were you to use the coins, you would shake three coins in your cupped hands and throw them onto a flat surface. Because you cannot know how they will land, you also have exceeded the capacity of your rational mind to control the outcome.

In that regard, the two methods, coins and yarrow stalks, use the same principle of activating the unconscious.

However, the coin method is inaccurate because the mathematical odds of obtaining a 6 or a 9 are equal, as are the odds of obtaining a 7 or 8. Because the law of averages is a law of the Universe, the odds always work themselves out, providing just as many sixes as nines, just as many sevens as eights. The section below discusses why that is undesirable and will lead to inaccurate answers.

Because the coin method is quick and easy, it is highly popular. It is worth taking the time to understand why it is vastly inferior so that you will never use coins, even though they sometimes appear to have provided a correct answer.

THE STATISTICS

Both the coin method and the yarrow stalk method yield lines numerically. The final numbers obtainable with both methods are 6, 7, 8, and 9. The following tables show the probabilities of obtaining those numbers with both methods. In the coin method, the lowest common denominator has not been used so the comparison can be more easily seen.

YARROW STALK METHOD	COIN METHOD
6 = 1 in 16	6 = 2 in 16
9 = 3 in 16	9 = 2 in 16
7 = 5 in 16	7 = 6 in 16
8 = 7 in 16	8 = 6 in 16

As you can see, with the coins, the probability of obtaining a 6 or a 9 is equal, but with the yarrow stalks, the probability of obtaining a 9 is three times greater than obtaining a six. That is highly favorable and vitally important since 9 is a strong, light-giving, beneficial line, while 6 is a weak, dark, generally unbeneficial line (although either type of line can be beneficial or unbeneficial according to its position in the kua).

Most importantly, manipulating the yarrow stalks, which takes about fifteen minutes to accomplish, engages you in spiritual communion with All-That-Is, which is the heart and soul of the process. The coin method takes less than one minute. If you want accurate answers, use yarrow stalks.

YARROW STALKS*

The ancients said that the stalk of the yarrow had a special spiritual nature and was therefore suitable for divination. Yarrow, also called "milfoil," grows in many places in the world. A book on plant life, obtainable in any library, will reveal where yarrow grows. It can be picked while it is still flowering and laid aside to dry, or it can be harvested after the flowers have turned brown and the stalks have dried. You can obtain seeds from a catalog or nursery and grow your own. Some New Age bookstores sell packages of yarrow stalks. The stalks should be anywhere from seven to thirteen inches long, relatively straight, and fairly smooth.

OTHER STALKS

Other stalks may be used but only until you can obtain yarrow stalks. Many plants have stalks similar to yarrow and

*Power Press imports yarrow stalks from China. The stalks are handpicked by farmers in northeast China specifically for use in divination with the I Ching. To order, write, call, or e-mail Power Press using the contact information on page iv.

can be used temporarily. The stalks must be relatively straight and fairly smooth, between seven and thirteen inches long. Most supermarkets sell packages of bamboo skewers. Fireplace matches with the match heads cut off can be used, but you may have to use sandpaper to make the matchsticks smooth and round.

Your attitude while manipulating any kind of stalks is of great importance. You must be calm and collected within yourself. Sincerity is essential.

ITEMS REQUIRED FOR ASKING QUESTIONS

- *The I Ching: The Book of Answers*
- Fifty yarrow stalks
- Paper and pen
- Incense
- A piece of silk in which to wrap the *The I Ching: The Book of Answers* when it is not being used
- A cord to tie the yarrow stalks together when they are not in use

PREPARATION

In divination, you must be motivated by what is honorable, correct, and virtuous. The law of cause and effect is absolute.

Every action produces a result, and the result is always in perfect accord with the action. If you are not as you should be, even the best opportunity and counsel will come to nothing. The hard lessons you learn for not being as you should be are not a form of punishment, but are for the purpose of guiding you onto the correct path.

Find a quiet place where you can be alone and undisturbed. Because this is an inquiry that probes the heart of the most spiritual essence of the Universe, reverence is appropriate.

At all times, treat and handle the objects used for divination as sacred. They should not be tossed about, but handled carefully. Perhaps you have a favorite blanket or mat to spread out, upon which you will place yourself and your objects of divination, or, if the mat or blanket is small, only your objects of divination. Whatever place you choose, be comfortable.

Light the incense and pass all the objects being used in the divination through the smoke three times, one at a time, in a circular, clockwise motion, beginning with your hand. Write the date, time, and location of your inquiry on the paper. Write your question and pass it through the smoke three times. If you are using my *I Ching Workbook*, pass the entire book through the smoke three times.

In my own preparation for asking questions, I softly beat an octagonal drum I made. On each of the eight wooden sides of the drum is burned in one of the eight trigrams. On the opposite sides of the wood, the inverse trigram is burned.

While I beat the drum, I call upon Fu Hsi and thank him for his wonderful system. I call upon King Wen and his son Tan, who helped in the creation of the I Ching, and thank them for their contribution. I thank Confucius for his contribution and also all those who have helped to bring this wonderful system through the ages for our use today. I ask them all to attend my quest. I ask them to please excuse my ignorance and to overlook my many shortcomings. I ask for their assistance.

THE YARROW STALK METHOD

Fifty yarrow stalks are used. One is symbolically laid aside and plays the role of observer until your inquiry is completed. You will find it helpful to follow the illustrations that accompany this section. Because there is a spiritual value in laying aside the observer stalk, I always pick it up at the end of my inquiry and thank it for its participation, and I thank the venerable ancient sages for their presence and assistance. The most important spiritual quality one can develop is that of reverence for all things. All-That-Is is aware of you, and your reverence shows that you are aware of All-That-Is.

Carefully follow the eleven steps of dividing the yarrow stalks as shown in the following illustrations:

1. Hold the bundle of forty-nine stalks in your left hand. Think about your question and the circumstances that gave rise to the question. If the question has to do with a person, visualize that person. If a problem is the subject of your inquiry, think about the various aspects of the problem. See in your mind's eye the people or objects associated with the question. Close your eyes and hold the question in your mind.

2. With your right hand, grasp a portion of stalks from the bundle held in your left hand. Open your eyes.

3. Place the bundle you have grasped in your right hand on the blanket and take from it one stalk.

4. Place that stalk between the little finger and ring finger of your left hand.

5. With your right hand, take bundles of four stalks from those remaining in your left hand until four or fewer stalks remain.

6. Place those four or fewer stalks between the ring finger and middle finger of your left hand.

7. Take the remaining stalks that were in your left hand and lay them down separately, retaining the stalks between your fingers.

8. Pick up the bundle of stalks that you first removed from your left hand and return that bundle to your left hand.

9. With your right hand, remove bundles of four until there are four or fewer stalks remaining.

10. Place those four or fewer stalks between your middle finger and your index finger and place the remaining stalks on the blanket, retaining the stalks placed between your fingers.

11. Count the stalks held between your fingers.

You must have either nine or five stalks. If you have any other number of stalks, you have either taken bundles of four incorrectly or you did not begin with the correct number of stalks. The various possibilities of stalks held between your fingers are:

$$1 - 4 - 4 = 9$$
$$1 - 1 - 3 = 5$$
$$1 - 3 - 1 = 5$$
$$1 - 2 - 2 = 5$$

As you can see, it is much more probable that you will obtain five stalks than nine stalks.

Nine stalks receive the numerical value of 2, and five stalks receive the numerical value of 3. Therefore, if your total number of stalks is nine, write the number 2 on your page as shown in the example on page 46. If the total number of stalks is five, write the number 3. Those nine or five stalks are now laid aside for the time being.

Repeat steps 1 through 11.

When you have gone through the eleven steps the second time, you must have either eight or four stalks remaining between your fingers. Any other number of stalks means that you have manipulated the stalks incorrectly or have dropped one or more stalks.

If you find that you have manipulated the stalks incorrectly, but you still hold the stalks between your fingers, restore the stalks to their respective bundles and count again. If you no longer hold the stalks between your fingers, you must repeat that division of the stalks, but just for that one operation. The first counting, which resulted in nine or five stalks, is still valid.

In the second grasping, the possible combinations of stalks held between your fingers are:

$$1 - 4 - 3 = 8$$
$$1 - 3 - 4 = 8$$
$$1 - 1 - 2 = 4$$
$$1 - 2 - 1 = 4$$

As you can see, the odds of obtaining four or eight stalks are equal. The four or eight stalks are laid aside near the bundle of nine or five stalks previously laid aside. Eight stalks receive the numerical value of 2. Four stalks receive the numerical value of 3. Write the correct number alongside the first number you wrote.

Repeat steps one through eleven.

At the completion of this third division of the yarrow stalks, you must either have a total of four or eight stalks. Any other total means you have counted incorrectly. As in the last division, eight stalks receive the numerical value of 2, and four stalks receive the numerical value of 3. Write the correct number alongside the other two numbers. All of the stalks, except for the observer stalk, may now be gathered together.

Total the three numbers you wrote. The result must be 6, 7, 8, or 9 as follows:

9 [2] + 8 [2] + 8 [2] = 6

5 [3] + 8 [2] + 8 [2] = 7
9 [2] + 8 [2] + 4 [3] = 7
9 [2] + 4 [3] + 8 [2] = 7

9 [2] + 4 [3] + 4 [3] = 8
5 [3] + 4 [3] + 8 [2] = 8
5 [3] + 8 [2] + 4 [3] = 8

5 [3] + 4 [3] = 4 [3] = 9

You now are able to record the first line of your kua, which is the Bottom Line. The following numbers yield the following lines:

$$6 = \text{— —} \cdot$$
$$7 = \text{———}$$
$$8 = \text{— —}$$
$$9 = \text{———} \cdot$$

The dots after the lines formed by the 6 and the 9 indicate that they are lines that move and should be taken into consideration in the answer to your question. Lines obtained with the numbers 7 or 8 are not to be taken into consideration in your answer. (Traditionally, to indicate that a line moves, an O was placed in the middle of a solid line and an X was placed in the middle of a broken line, but I find that practice confusing and so have adopted the method of placing a dot at the end of any moving line, whether it is solid or broken.)

To obtain the other five lines, repeat the above process five more times. Because the kua is built from the bottom up, when you record the numbers for each succeeding line, write them above the first three numbers from which the first line was obtained.

As you saw in the example, a line that is obtained with a 6 or a 9 changes into its opposite: broken lines into solid lines and solid lines into broken lines. The changing line or lines give rise to a new kua that shows what the situation will develop into or will further clarify the answer given in the first kua. None of the lines of the second kua are to be taken into consideration, not even the corresponding moving lines that were in the first kua, although you may read all the lines to gain a better understanding of the kua.

At first, manipulating the stalks to obtain a kua will take considerable time, but after a while the handling of the stalks becomes natural, and the process goes much faster. Be patient, perform the manipulation of the stalks correctly, record your results accurately, and you will find the results to be extremely gratifying and worthwhile.

FINDING YOUR KUA

After you have formed the six lines of your kua, refer to page 403, where you will find a chart of the sixty-four kua.

The chart shows the eight trigrams in a row across the top of the chart and again in a column down the left side. Find the upper trigram (the top three lines) of your kua in the top row and the lower trigram (the bottom three lines) in the left-side column. Then follow the columns down and across until the extended lines of the trigrams intersect. In that square, you will see the number of the kua for which you are searching. The number of the page on which the kua can be found is printed in the upper portion of the same square. The sixty-four kua, taken as whole, comprise one movement from its beginning to its end—a complete cycle with 384 steps.

Through the manipulation of the yarrow stalks, you can discover which kua pertains to your question. The kua depicts the condition or situation that relates to your question. You can change that condition into any other condition by taking the appropriate steps, steps which you will discover in the I Ching answers. As you continue to use the I Ching for guidance, you will become ever stronger, your character will improve, and you will learn the laws of the Universe and how to use them for your best benefit and the benefit of those around you.

Remember, for accurate interpretation, the moving lines, if any, take precedence over the meaning of the kua. For instance, in Kua 41, "Decrease," the kua depicts a time of general decrease. Line 5 of the same kua says, "In this time of decrease, you will be greatly increased." Even though the kua depicts a time of decrease, Line 5 says that you will be greatly increased, and because the line takes precedence over the kua, you will be greatly increased.

KUA 41

If you obtain more than one moving line, remember that the action starts with the moving line closest to the bottom and proceeds upward from moving line to moving line.

Remember also to disregard nonmoving lines. The first moving line is closer to the present, and later moving lines depict later times.

STORING THE DIVINATION OBJECTS

Traditionally, all the items used in divination, such as the *The I Ching: The Book of Answers* and the yarrow stalks, should be kept in a spiritually proper place such as on a mantle or a special shelf or in a cabinet, all of which should be above shoulder level.

The yarrow stalks should be tied together in a bundle to prevent loss of a stalk and to provide strength for all the stalks. *The I Ching: The Book of Answers* and the stalks should be wrapped separately in silk.

A FEW SUGGESTIONS

Until you have grown accustomed to relying on the I Ching, you may find it difficult to approach it with any great degree of determination to follow its counsel. When you have learned through experience to trust in its guidance, you will have discovered a rare treasure indeed, and you will be able to act confidently upon its counsel.

You will find it remarkably rewarding to set aside some time on your birthdays to ask, "What can I expect from this birthday year?" Or, "What do I have to pay attention to in order to have the most productive birthday year?"

Similarly, on the first day of the new year, you can ask, "What does the new year hold in store for me?" Or, "What can I do to have the most productive new year?" Married couples can take the occasion of their anniversary to ask, "What can we do to strengthen our marriage this year?" Each partner should also inquire individually because each one may need improvement in a different area.

You will find it helpful to ask questions regarding almost any issue or concern—health, financial matters, social situations, business decisions, trips, undertakings of any kind, philosophical questions, and questions about people, events, and conditions. Your questions can be about the past, the present, or the future.

Using the I Ching will enable you to see into the heart of every matter, but you will never be given information that would cause you harm or would cause you to act in a way that would not be in your best interest. Good questions are those that will help you to improve yourself, such as, "What can I do to improve myself?" Or, "Why am I unhappy?" Or, "Why can't I get ahead?" Or better yet, "What can I do to improve myself so I can get ahead?"

Because all change is subject to universal law, if you use the I Ching, which is based on the interplay of the universal laws, you can see when situations begin to disintegrate and spiral out of control. If you catch them at their beginnings, you can take preventive action. Left unattended, conditions can grow to such proportions that no action you take will prevent failure.

The questions are endless, the answers are perfect, and everything is formulated so that you can accomplish your mission on Earth to perfect yourself as a Divine Being.

Remember, you are a golden child of an eternal Universe. You are blessed completely.

part five
THE KUA

1
CH'IEN

Creating

THE KUA

This is the kua of creating yourself as an individual or of creating some idea that you have conceived. Receiving this kua is indeed a blessing, for this is the kua of Heaven, in which all the lines are strong, good, and virtuous, and it guarantees sublime success from the primal depths of the Universe, provided that you act in accordance with its provisions. It is rare to receive this kua as an answer, but when you do, you are faced with an opportunity of the greatest magnitude. When your success is guaranteed from the primal depths of the Universe, it means that even the spiritual world will come to your aid and that blessings will be heaped upon you. Confucius, the great Chinese sage and I Ching scholar, said that when Heaven blesses us, it helps us, and to be helped by Heaven is to be helped indeed.

However, to achieve the success you seek you must act with the utmost integrity and honor. This means putting yourself in accord with the six lines of this kua, all of which are pure, light-giving, powerful, and just.

If you do not, the enormous potential promised by this kua will not be achieved. Examine yourself closely to see if you have any bad habits or bad intentions that could potentially hurt yourself or your plan. If you find areas in your character that can be improved, start the corrective work immediately. That is the key to unlocking your full potential and the full potential of your plan or of what you are conceiving.

Because this kua unfolds over time, it also requires perseverance and endurance: perseverance in a course of action that is right, good, and just; and endurance to see things through to the end. If you act with complete integrity and honor, you will bring into existence the full power of this kua and experience sublime success. You will fulfill this kua's great promise: you will mount to the skies of success as though on the wings of six dragons!

THE LINES

BOTTOM LINE: Your intentions are good and you are in a position of strength, but it is too early to act. Other events are developing that will make the great success of your plan possible, but these have not yet come about. Keep yourself, your plan, or what you are creating secret for now. While you wait for the right conditions to emerge, cultivate yourself and refine your plan or creation. Examine yourself to see if you have any character traits or tendencies that you can improve.

Remember, this is the kua of Heaven and of the highest achievement, so every aspect of your being must be impeccable. Review your project or plan carefully to make certain that it is in accord with the highest principles. Practice being calm and patient.

If you act prematurely, you will only waste your energy without gaining anything. Your success is assured, but only if you remain true to what is highest and best within you.

LINE 2: The time is at hand when you can begin to achieve your great success. Set to work. You need help, so seek out a teacher or an expert in the field. Your greatness, or that of your plan or creation, is now becoming apparent. Promote yourself or your plan with great enthusiasm. The Universe has blessed you with a great gift in this opportunity for success. You deserve it, but it is only through right action, according to the highest principles, that you will claim it. Work hard, and your efforts will be well rewarded.

LINE 3: The opportunity for your success is at hand. At this time, you must exert your maximum effort.

You have good intentions and are in a position of overall strength, you are also at a dangerous point of transition that requires extreme caution and attention to detail. Because you have so much to accomplish, you must be tireless in your efforts. Above all, continue to act with complete integrity.

LINE 4: Success is immediately before you, but not yet within your grasp. Continue to persevere, and do not feel discouraged by failure. Perseverance and endurance are essential: perseverance in acting with complete integrity, and endurance in seeing your creation through to the end. This is not yet the moment of your ultimate success, but that time is coming. If you remain unwaveringly true to the highest principles, you will achieve the success promised by this kua. You should now spend some time contemplating whether you really want to achieve worldly success, or whether your true path is to lead a life of quiet solitude in which you focus on developing yourself. Either way, you will be successful.

LINE 5: Congratulations! You have arrived at the pinnacle of success. Be content with what you have achieved. If you try to expand your success further at this time, you will only attract failure. All things, when they reach their maximum potential, inevitably turn toward their opposite. Success turns to failure, and fullness to emptiness. Therefore, do not seek to increase your success. Instead, share it with others. Ordinary people seldom think about sharing their good fortune, but if you do so, you will experience long-lasting prosperity. Also, it is essential that you continue to examine yourself or your creation so you are sure that you are acting in accord with all that is highest and best within you.

TOP LINE: You have carried your success too far and have caused it to begin transforming into decline. You will regret your arrogance. Do what you can to make amends and to retreat to your former position of success. Consider this setback a learning experience that will prepare you for future times of success that will come to you. Continue improving yourself in as many ways you can. Everything that happens benefits you. Remain cheerful, and be thankful for the good things that you still possess.

NOTE

If all the lines are moving, this kua turns into the second kua, K'un, "Open, Receptive, Yielding, Willing to Follow." The blending of these two kua, power and submissiveness, is indeed great. Therefore, gentle and persistent action will lead to good fortune.

2
K'UN

Open, Receptive, Yielding, Willing to Follow

THE KUA

Sublime success will come to you if you are willing to follow good advice, are open and receptive to new information, yield to others' ideas and wishes, follow wise leaders who have worthy goals, work hard, cooperate, and avoid taking on leadership. If you try to lead, you will go astray and will fail to achieve the sublime success promised in this kua. Seek out like-minded people to help you, and, if you find them, join with them or have them join with you, but do not attempt to lead them. If you must carry on alone, do so, but seek guidance all the same.

You will enjoy the sublime success promised by this kua only if you adhere strictly to its attributes, which are receptive, yielding, submissive, and willing to follow. Avoid arrogance.

The Universe supports those who are modest and brings down those who are arrogant. If you are the leader, fulfill your duties of leadership, but not without following the advice of those who can offer you wise counsel. Seek information from every source, ask for help, and trust your advisors. This is a time when following rather than leading will benefit you most. The success promised by this kua is "sublime," meaning that it is not only success in terms of abundance, but also success that is endowed with greatness of spirit and therefore benefits the whole of the people.

THE LINES

BOTTOM LINE: If you hope to reach the end you desire, you must take great care at the beginning. Openness and receptiveness are especially important because you are just at the start. Caution is also essential. This line indicates that the situation has already begun to disintegrate. If you do not stop this destructive process, harmful consequences will result. If you are trying to lead, stop immediately.

Seek advice about how to proceed from someone you trust. Do not rely on yourself, or you will go astray. To succeed, you must follow advice and be open to new ideas. If you are the leader, fulfill your duties of leadership, but rely on your trusted advisors for guidance.

LINE 2: You are in a key position to fulfill your own aims or the aims of your allies. To achieve sublime success, give up harboring any ulterior motives, remain true to your highest principles, and do all you can to fulfill your own goals and those of your associates. Seek advice. Always keep in mind the attributes of this kua, and remain open, receptive, yielding, and willing to follow. They are your guiding principles, and only by adhering to them will you accomplish your goal.

LINE 3: Great modesty and conscientiousness are now essential and will be rewarded with sublime success and good fortune. Modesty means that you must cultivate a humble attitude and avoid giving yourself airs, stop trying to impress others, and do not boast about what you have accomplished. Conscientiousness means that you fulfill your tasks and obligations with the utmost care.

If you are fortunate enough to occupy an important position but still remain modest and conscientious, you will shine like the sun at midday, and no one will hold your success against you. Also, you will attain your goals quickly and easily. If you are in a subordinate position but remain modest and conscientious, you will be rewarded with recognition, gifts, and rapid advancement through the ranks. Downplay your talents, and avoid claiming credit for the role you have played or will play.

Stay focused on your only goal, which is to complete the task at hand in a state of openness and receptivity. If you follow the advice of this line now, abundant success and honor will be yours later.

LINE 4: You have almost attained your goal. Beware of becoming intoxicated with your achievements. If you allow yourself to become overly excited about your approaching success, you may grow careless, and fail to pay attention to crucial matters, and thereby ruin your chances for success. It is precisely at the point when success is at hand that you must remain most cautious. By maintaining the attitude and course of action that have brought you to this point, you will arrive at your goal surely and safely. Remain even more modest, reserved, and cautious than ever, for danger looms. Challenging or confronting those who oppose you will only earn their hostility. Continue working to bring matters to their conclusion, but do not try to claim credit. Once your success is at hand, avoid obvious displays of triumph or celebration. Instead, remain calm and low-key. In that way, you will achieve your sublime success.

LINE 5: You are in the best possible position. Still, you must remain modest. Downplay the advantages you enjoy, whether these be talent, beauty, riches, or powerful connections. When you are prospering, it is important that you possess enough greatness of spirit to bear with and forgive others' failings. Just as water washes clean whatever it touches, so too must you, as a superior person, pardon mistakes and forgive even intentional transgressions. By doing so, you will guarantee the upward spiral of your prosperity. Inferior people cannot resist the opportunity to chastise others, but, when they do, they incur resentment, destroy unanimity, crush the enthusiasm of their associates, and destroy their own chances for success. Be content with what you have achieved. If you follow this guidance, you will achieve the sublime success promised in this kua.

TOP LINE: You have become controlling and adversarial. That will result in injury for all concerned. To minimize the damage, make whatever amends you can. Also, seek advice from a qualified person, and follow the advice you receive.

3
CHUN

Difficulty and Danger at the Beginning

THE KUA

All beginnings require exceptional care if they are to result in a great harvest. In the beginning, everything needed for complete fulfillment is present but not yet in its proper place, so a state of confusion exists. It is not necessary that you have everything you need at the outset, for at the appointed time, it will all come: money, helpers, events, material assistance, and opportunities. The only necessity is your firm determination to reach your goal.

Here at the beginning, danger is present, so avoid taking immediate action. You must wait, and, during this waiting period, seek out helpers. Also, use this time to organize and develop a plan that you can begin to follow, but remain open and willing to rework it if you find that it needs adjustment.

By proceeding in that manner, you will avert danger. You will also bring order out of the confusion of this time of beginning and will thus manifest supreme success.

THE LINES

BOTTOM LINE: An obstacle awaits you at the very beginning. Although you have the strength needed to push ahead, stop and wait. Consolidate your position. Refine your plan. Find helpers from among the common people. In general, this kind of obstruction takes the form of opposition, but, if you are a wise and intelligent person, you can turn this to your advantage.

Foolish and unknowledgeable people are ignorant of the laws of the Universe, so they bewail their fate when they encounter opposition. They blame circumstances or other people and, refusing to take responsibility for their circumstances, abandon their efforts. However, if you know the laws of the Universe, you can use opposition and obstacles to gather strength, improve yourself, and adopt a more useful and effective course of action. Opposition or obstacles are often guideposts that point us in a better direction. People of true understanding take each ounce of adversity and turn it to their advantage. Because danger is present at this time, examine the obstacle indicated by this line to determine whether it is warning you to change course or revise your plan. Do not abandon your goal, but hold it clearly in your mind and maintain a firm determination to reach it. Be cautious, and have confidence that success will be yours in the end. If you maintain this attitude toward opposition and obstacles, your strength will grow like a young bear's, and you will reach your goals as though on the back of Pegasus himself.

LINE 2: Both the obstacles and the dangers are increasing. Your plan is falling apart. A powerful person wants to help you, but because you are facing so many obstacles and difficulties, you do not trust that person. Later, it will become evident that this person is sincere, but you will wait for a long time before accepting this alliance. Continue with your plan, for the setbacks you are experiencing are only temporary. If you persevere and endure, you will win in the end.

LINE 3: Impatience sets in. You have failed to obtain expert guidance and have plunged ahead, only to find yourself lost in difficulties because you lack the needed strength and knowledge. Stop and retreat. To continue will only lead to more setbacks. Revise your plan. Seek help from a qualified person. Ask for assistance with advice or resources. Be patient. Success will come, but you need help.

LINE 4: You encounter another obstacle, but because you hold an important position of trust, you must move forward. You have an opportunity to join forces with someone who can help you. Seize this opportunity, whatever the cost, and move forward. If you take timely and appropriate action, you will experience good fortune, and everything that happens will benefit you.

LINE 5: You are in the position of leadership but lack the strength needed to carry out your plans or to fulfill your intentions of benefiting others. Furthermore, you cannot expect help from anyone else. At this time, a small additional effort to move toward your goal will bring you good fortune, but an all-out effort will bring only failure. Be satisfied with the small gains possible at this time. If you attempt too much, you may lose what you have. The ancient wisdom states that those who attempt too much end by succeeding in nothing.

TOP LINE: The difficulties increase, and, because you lack sufficient strength, they are too much for you to overcome at this time. You feel great sadness and regret. Focus on learning all the lessons you can from this experience, and move on. Other opportunities await you. Keep in mind that you are a golden child of an eternal Universe of which you are an inseparable part. In the end, everything that happens benefits you. The Universe will not permit it to be otherwise.

4
MÊNG

Inexperience

THE KUA

When inexperienced persons seek guidance from experienced teachers, they meet with success because it is the teacher's joy and responsibility to teach others. It is important, though, that students have the right attitude toward their teachers. These are some basic guidelines that will help.

First, students must say that they are inexperienced and need guidance.

Second, they should be modest and show the teacher proper respect.

Third, they should never mistrustfully question the teacher more than once about the same question. However, if the answer is truly not understood, additional questions are permissible. Following these simple steps will make the teacher happy to cooperate, and thus the student will continue to learn. This then becomes an amazing time for students because they can learn the great words of wisdom and become an expert in their chosen field. That is how teachers lead their students to success.

If you are the teacher and your students continue to doubt your answers or do not show you the respect you deserve, it is wise to abandon your efforts. Some people are not ready to listen to the wise words of a sage. Instead, let them go out in the world, where the Universe will give them what they need for their learning. Over time, they will be molded, shaped, and changed to the point where they will be more willing to listen. There is no saying how long this will take, for it is different with everyone.

This kua offers advice for both students and teachers. You must think about the question you asked and decide which one you are. Once you have decided, follow the guidance appropriate for your role.

THE LINES

BOTTOM LINE: Teaching the inexperienced often requires strict discipline. Teachers who free their students from the bondage of misinformation and false assumptions bring success and honor to both themselves and their students. However, if students fail to respond to the discipline of learning, teachers must turn to other means of instruction. If they persist in trying to discipline unwilling students, the only result will be an end to the relationship. The failure of a student is always the failure of the teacher, and anyone who refuses to admit this is as far off the track as the other. If you see yourself as the student in this question, honor your teacher, pay great attention to the teachings you receive, and study hard. Then you will be rewarded and will progress quickly toward your goal. If you are the teacher, be patient and strict but not harsh. In teaching, patience and repetition are the keys to success.

Knowledge is the key to the wealth of the Universe. Thus, when you know how to earn a living, you will never be poor; when you know how to care for your health, you will rarely be ill; when you know how to occupy yourself, you will never be bored—and when you follow the path of the superior person, misfortune, failure, and suffering will pass you by.

LINE 2: Teaching inexperienced students with gentleness, as well as patience with their ignorance and errors, brings success and good fortune. Knowing know how to function harmoniously with persons of the other sex brings good fortune; tolerance, patience, love, and understanding are the keys to harmony. Give responsibility for the household, organization, or project to those children or administrators who are in harmony with you.

LINE 3: If you abandon your values in the hope of becoming a favorite or gaining some advantage with people of wealth and power, you will be of little value to yourself or others. Whatever temporary gains you may achieve will not be worth the loss of your dignity and self-respect. This is not to say that you should never cultivate strong relationships with people of rank or merit, but rather that you should not demean yourself, flatter, or compromise your values to gain favor.

LINE 4: Stubborn, rebellious students who refuse to accept their mentors' teachings or advice should be abandoned and left to experience the strictest discipline of all, that of the Universe, which will dispense those teachings through harsh experience. Those hard lessons will bring shame and humiliation in their wake. If you are the student, offer your apologies to your teacher, mentor, parent, or guide, and immediately adopt a more respectful and attentive attitude. You have gone astray and are about to be left to your own devices. That will have negative consequences.

If you are the teacher, make one final attempt to reach your student, but if he or she rejects what you have to offer, turn your back and leave everything in the hands of the Universe. Students who refuse to listen to their teachers will inevitably learn by experiencing the harsh consequences of their own folly.

LINE 5: The subject of this line is humble, willing to learn, and respectful to teachers. Such people are sure to meet with the approval of their teachers and with good fortune in the world. If you are the teacher, congratulations, for you have earned your student's respect and compliance, and this reflects great honor on you both. If you are the student, congratulations as well, for your teacher or mentor respects and admires you, and the Universe, which loves a willing and respectful student, will shower you with rewards.

TOP LINE: The person represented by this line requires punishment to correct his or her faults and to avert further errors. Punishment is never an end in itself but rather a corrective measure. Any punishment that exceeds what is required to prevent a recurrence will have negative effects.

If you are the inexperienced person, you have brought shame on yourself and on your teacher or mentor. Your actions have demonstrated that you do not understand how the Universe works or life in general. At this point on your path to enlightenment, you do not deserve any recognition or success. Accept any punishment that comes to you as justified. Correct your faults and learn from your experience. If you are the teacher, impose whatever punishment is necessary to correct your student's shortcomings. If this fails, leave your student to his or her folly.

5
HSÜ

Holding Back in the Face of Danger

THE KUA

You are a strong person who desires to advance, but grave danger threatens your advance. The correct action is to wait until the danger passes, for to advance in the face of such danger would be foolhardy. Because the lower trigram, which represents you, is composed of three strong, solid lines, you will ultimately be successful, provided you remain true to the nature of the three solid lines, which are light-giving, pure, and virtuous.

If you fail to wait, the danger that looms will overwhelm you, and you will not attain your goal. However, after the time of waiting is past, you will benefit from moving toward your goal again. During this time of waiting, you should refine your plans, enjoy relaxation and recreation, maintain a joyous and promising outlook, and remain unconcerned, knowing that you will ultimately reach your goal. Do not waste this time in empty hoping. Instead, let yourself be filled with the inner certainty that ultimate success lies ahead. If you allow yourself to doubt, you will only fall prey to worry, anxiety, and fear-filled imaginings about the future, all of which will be damaging to your future success and will cause you stress. Be confident that you will reach your goal, and you will enjoy happy, peaceful thoughts and will engage in useful activities, both of which lead directly to success. By acting in accordance with what is highest and best within you will you achieve success and good fortune.

THE LINES

BOTTOM LINE: You are in a strong position, and you have the support of those above you. The danger that approaches is not yet at hand. Nevertheless, you must wait until it passes completely before moving forward. Meanwhile, focus on developing and strengthening your character, for only your good character and complete integrity will see you through to the end without blame attaching to your progress.

LINE 2: The danger draws nearer, but you are strong and in an important position. Still, this is not a time to act. Wait for a more favorable moment to move forward. Your associates may engage in petty gossip that you may find hurtful, but, in the end, good fortune will come if you act with integrity.

LINE 3: Instead of waiting, as the situation required, you have made an untimely start that has left you vulnerable to the danger that threatens. Retreat if you can, and wait for a more favorable time before attempting to move forward. Make whatever corrections are possible, and hope for the best. Always keep in mind that you must act with integrity if you are to succeed at all.

LINE 4: You are in a high position, but weak, and the danger that has been threatening is finally at hand. No help is forthcoming. You are on your own. The situation is desperate, and you must take immediate action. Do whatever is necessary to save yourself, but be sure that you assess the situation correctly.

It may be that the best course of action is to halt your attempts to advance and to lie low as you wait for the danger to pass. Do not be aggressive or forceful, for that will only heighten the danger. Be yielding and submissive. If you do not resist, the danger will probably pass you by.

LINE 5: You are strong and in a place of leadership. Even though danger surrounds you, you have confidence in your own strength and resources and are therefore comfortable

enough to relax and not let the danger upset you. If you persevere in a path of integrity and remain confident, good fortune will come to you

TOP LINE: The time for waiting is over. The danger is
at hand. When danger is so extreme, there is usually little
hope, but an unforeseen stroke of good fortune in the form
of help from an unexpected quarter comes your way.

6
SUNG

Argument, Dispute, Conflict, Adversaries

THE KUA

You are sincere but are nonetheless entangled in an argument. Remain calm and clearheaded so that you are always ready to meet your opponent halfway and to work toward arriving at a settlement. No conflict should ever be allowed to become long-lasting. If you remain open to resolving the dispute, good fortune will come. However, if you insist on prolonging it, the outcome will be misfortune. Even if you win the argument, hostility will linger if you fail to reach a friendly solution. The correct action is to settle things peacefully because this will end the danger. You would do well to seek guidance from a qualified person and then set out to accomplish a great aim. Be sure to plan this endeavor with great care, for achieving your goal will benefit you far more than involving yourself in a conflict.

THE LINES

BOTTOM LINE: A superior force confronts you. Make every effort to end the conflict. There will be some gossip, but that will soon die away, and good fortune will prevail in the end. Prolonging this dispute will bring only misfortune. Your position is weak, and your strength is not equal to the task; therefore, continuing this conflict will be foolhardy. End it now, and good fortune will come.

LINE 2: You are strong, but your opponent is even stronger. Continuing the dispute will result in unfortunate consequences; therefore, retreat will bring good fortune and will also keep your friends and associates from being drawn into the struggle. Only the foolhardy contend with superior forces. Free yourself from this situation as quickly and easily as you can, and good fortune will be yours.

LINE 3: You may have or soon might experience a loss of some kind or there is a possibility that someone may challenge you for something you own. Perhaps someone is seeking or soon will seek to take credit for an accomplishment that rightfully belongs to you. There is some danger in the situation, so you must be alert for the danger. If you experience a loss or receive a challenge, take heart, for what is truly your own will remain your own, and because of that, good fortune comes in the end. It will benefit you to follow a path of high integrity and work at brightening your already bright virtue by studying the wisdom of the great sages.

If you are in someone's service, accomplish your work just for the sake of achieving the common goal without expectation of reward or credit.

LINE 4: Avoid engaging in arguments for the time being because they will bring only failure in their wake. Retreat from your position, and accept what befalls you as the best possible result for now. Only if you cultivate and maintain this attitude of acceptance will good fortune come to you. According to Universal law, everything that happens benefits us. Even if an event appears unfavorable at first, this is merely an outward appearance that conceals its completely favorable and beneficial aspects, which you will eventually come to realize. Accept all that happens as intended for your complete benefit, and it will be so. You will also save the time spent in lamenting an event that was always for your benefit.

LINE 5: Although your opponent is cooperative, you cannot successfully resolve the conflict yourselves. Take your argument before a judge, arbiter, or someone in authority who can settle the dispute. If you do, supreme good fortune will result. Be open and willing to settle this disagreement. Meet your opponent at least halfway. To continue the argument will bring misfortune to all concerned.

TOP LINE: You have carried the dispute too far. Even if you win, you will not be victorious, for everything that is obtained by force must be maintained by force, and this requires constant, exhausting vigilance. Having forced your victory on your opponent, the hostility between you will only persist, and you will find yourself attacked again and again. Find some way to make peace with the other side, even if you must give up part of what you have won. You will be better off in the end.

7
SHIH

Collective Forces

THE KUA

This kua represents the power of people working together to accomplish something great. It is a wonderful time because the people will gladly rally around you and your cause. During this time, you can and should rely on the people for their help in accomplishing your goal. Encourage them to help you, for they are your friends and allies and will prove to be very valuable. For the group to be effective, you must provide clear-cut and worthy goals to which they can dedicate themselves. This will awaken their enthusiasm. Shower your helpers with praise, be generous and loving, and show them how much you appreciate their help. Doing that will keep your helpers motivated and will thus keep their support. With their help, you will make much greater progress than you can alone.

THE LINES

BOTTOM LINE: In this time of beginning, as in all beginnings, you must proceed with exceptional care if the desired end is to be reached. Order must prevail from the outset. Your plan must be clear and complete, your goal must be worthy, the group must be highly organized, and the resources you require must be in place. Because there is a certain weakness present in the situation, extra caution is required. Perhaps you should consult the oracle again to see in what ways you can better your chances for success.

LINE 2: You have been designated as the leader, and, if you have people above you, they have given you exclusive and total command. You should now be a strong presence in the midst of your people by encouraging them, helping them, sharing good and bad times with them, and, at the same time, providing strong guidance and leadership. If you fulfill all these responsibilities, you will be rewarded for your actions. Also, if you accept those honors modestly and in the name of those you are leading rather than taking all the credit yourself, your followers will love you for your unselfish actions, and no one will resent you or your leadership, and good fortune will be yours.

LINE 3: Leadership is either completely in the wrong hands, or a highly placed subordinate is undermining the leader. Disorder and danger are present. In either case, if the wrong leader is not removed or the sabotage is allowed to continue, defeat will result, and you will experience great misfortune. Take whatever action you can to correct the problem. Replace the leader, or track down the source of the undermining and stop it. You can prevent a total disaster, but you must take immediate action. However, if disaster does occur, take heart, for there will always be another day, another battle, or another opportunity. Learn from this defeat, move on, and be grateful for everything that still remains to you.

LINE 4: You are facing forces too great to overcome. Retreat is the only proper course of action at this time. This does not mean that you have lost your victory, but simply that a retreat is now called for. It will allow you to review your plans and strengthen your collective forces. An orderly retreat is not defeat, but rather a strategy that will gain you time to plan an effective counterattack.

LINE 5: You or your group are either under some form of attack, or opportunities are present that will allow you to gain an advantage or prize. If you are to succeed in either situation, the most experienced person available should be named as the sole leader of the group, and less-experienced members should be assigned to whatever positions make the best use of them. However, if you push further in your attack after fighting off your adversaries or after obtaining the advantage or prize, misfortune will result. Those who attempt too much end by succeeding in nothing.

TOP LINE: Congratulations, for you have or are about to achieve victory. Be sure to reward your loyal helpers well. Reward those who have shown the greatest integrity and highest moral values with positions of authority and influence and provide them with wealth. However, when it comes to helpers who have proven themselves loyal but are possibly of questionable integrity, give them money or other tangible rewards, but do not name them to positions of power or influence. Inferior people do not make good use of such positions, and, in the end, they usually turn their power and influence against those from whom it came.

8
PI

Joining,
Supporting, Uniting

THE KUA

This hexagram represents a time when you can easily gather people around you and form a group. The group can be as small as yourself and one other person or much larger. Each member brings strength to the group so that the group becomes strong and enduring.

Some people may hesitate to join with you, but eventually you will win them over. If they wait too long to join with you, they will incur misfortune because they will have missed their opportunity. For the group to be successful, it requires that you provide clear-cut goals around which everyone can rally. As the leader, you must be steadfast in maintaining your intention to reach your goals, you must adhere to good values, you must be loyal to the group, and you must hold the best interests of the group uppermost in your mind. To hold your group together and to inspire them, it is important that you possess greatness of spirit, enthusiasm, a positive attitude, strength, and wisdom.

Look to strengthening and improving your character so that you are always performing at optimum levels. Before you begin, inquire of the oracle again, and ask what you need to know to accomplish your goal. If you begin without being equal to the task, you will incur misfortune, and it would have been better for you and your followers that you had never attempted the union.

If you feel that you are not equal to the task, it will better for you to join some other organization or group of which you can be a part. The pronouncement of this kua is that forming a group or being part of a group will bring you good fortune.

THE LINES

BOTTOM LINE: You are just beginning, and you stand alone. Sincerity is of the utmost importance at this time because it will bring you good fortune from an unexpected source. Be on the lookout for that source. If you act out of hidden or devious motives, misfortune will follow. Success will come to you only if you are forthright, open, and dedicated to doing what is right and to acting for the group's benefit.

LINE 2: You hold a position of subordinate authority and have a good relationship with the leader. If you remain inwardly loyal to your leader and are cautious in your outward behavior, good fortune will prevail.

LINE 3: You are in a position to take a major step upward in your group, but you are associating with people of questionable integrity. However, because you are not in a position of power, and your superiors will not help you, the only way you can succeed is by severing your ties with those inferior people and supporting those in power. Do not be afraid. If you act in accord with this counsel, you will be successful.

LINE 4: You are close to those in power. Show your loyalty and support openly. Your subordinates will not support you, but if you persevere in visible demonstrations of loyalty that are rooted in your true intentions, success and good fortune will result.

LINE 5: You are in the place of leadership. It is essential that you continue to uphold the attributes mentioned in the opening paragraph of this kua. Accept and welcome those who wish to join with you, but do not pursue anyone who appears reluctant. If people whom you believe are important to your cause wish to depart, let them go. Your success is assured, and their nonparticipation is part of that. You are just and well intentioned, so no one need fear you. Good fortune is assured.

TOP LINE: You have waited too long, and the opportunity for joining, uniting, or supporting has come and gone. Even your good relationship with the leader will not help you now.

Misfortune lies ahead. Do not be dismayed. Instead, learn from this experience. Always keep in mind that great opportunities await you. Develop the attributes mentioned in this kua, and you will ultimately achieve great good fortune. Be grateful for the good things you still possess.

9
HSIAO CH'U

Gentle Restraint, Holding Back

THE KUA

The lower trigram of this kua is formed of three solid lines, whose movement is upward and represents a strong force that wants to advance. You may be the force, or it may be a group to which you belong. Your advance is being blocked by someone or something that is represented by the broken line in the fourth place. Because the fourth line is a weak, broken line, the force, which can be a person, group, or obstacle, is weak, and therefore, cannot permanently block you, but it can restrain your advance and hold it in check, though only for a short time. The brief period of holding back will be of great benefit because the future is being prepared for the time when you will be able to advance again. During this time of mild restraint, you should improve yourself in whatever ways you can so that when the gentle restraining force ceases, or you overcome it, you will be ready to move forward. If your question was about your taking action, the answer is that you should gently restrain yourself for the time being until a more appropriate time for advance appears.

THE LINES

BOTTOM LINE: You are strong and in a favorable position. Your strength and position have led you to begin your advance, but this is not the right course of action because the time for advance is not at hand.

If you continue, you will encounter an obstacle or person who will stop you. It is better to stop yourself rather than to be stopped by another. If you restrain yourself and wait for a more fortunate time to advance, which is coming, you will cause good fortune to ensue.

LINE 2: Because of your great strength and the position of influence you occupy, you have begun to advance. However, your advance is not in harmony with the time. If you push on, you will only find yourself lost in difficulties. Instead, restrain your advance at this time and wait for a more favorable time, which is coming. If you follow this guidance, you will experience good fortune.

LINE 3: You have acted so forcefully that you have caused a breakdown. As the ancient text says, "The spokes burst out of the wagon wheels." You expected a rapid and easy advance, but in this time of gentle restraint, such aggressiveness was doomed to failure.

Your behavior results in friction and arguments. Halt any attempt to advance, and make what amends you can.

LINE 4: You are in a position of trust, and you are responsible for gently restraining the strong advancing forces. Your task is to hold them in check for as long you can, even though they cannot be stopped permanently. Because you are in agreement with the leader, you will receive his or her support. If you remain focused on your task and sincere in your intentions, you will avoid a major battle, and fear will fade away.

If you fail to stop the opposing forces completely, no one will blame you because your task is simply to restrain them temporarily.

Thus, no one will criticize you for your actions, and your success will be rewarded.

LINE 5: You are strong and in a leadership position. You also have the loyalty of a gentle assistant. Do not hesitate to place your trust in that person. Together you will achieve wealth that you will both share. Do not try to accomplish anything great at this time because this is the time of gentle restraint. Satisfy yourself with accomplishing small goals for now because that is how you will eventually overcome the weak force that is holding you in check.

TOP LINE: The time of gentle restraint has done its work. You have achieved your goal. Pressing forward at this time will be foolhardy and will invite misfortune. Instead, take this time to rest and enjoy what you have achieved.

10
LÜ

Walking Your Path

THE KUA

This kua depicts you "treading on the tail of a tiger," meaning a powerful person or group who can cause you harm. However, even though you tread on the tiger's tail, it will not bite you because you are sincere and agreeable and know how to behave properly.

Such behavior brings you success. The key to your success lies in cultivating a pleasing and sincere personality, which will bring you success and good fortune because the person or group represented by the tiger will trust and respect you. Pleasant manners win over even bad-tempered people. If you do not let their unpleasantness irritate or upset you, your own pleasant manners will have a positive and calming effect on them. Receiving this kua as your answer foretells that you will have success if you accept the guidance of this kua.

THE LINES

BOTTOM LINE: You are strong and in a strong position, but the situation is just beginning to unfold, and you lack the support of those in power. If you act simply and modestly, and not impulsively, you will make progress and no one will criticize you. Be cautious and reserved. Above all, avoid offending anyone by your behavior. Any discourteous behavior or action on your part will work to your disadvantage. Also, because this is just the beginning, cultivate endurance to see you through to the end.

LINE 2: You are strong and occupy a strong and stable position of influence with your peers or associates. Still, moving forward forcefully at this time is not a wise course of action because you lack the support of those in authority. If you remain modest in your conduct and in the goals you set for yourself, you will make progress as if you are walking a smooth, level path.

Maintaining harmonious conduct is important. Remember, this is the kua of treading on the tail of the tiger. Be careful, cooperative, and courteous, and all will be well.

LINE 3: Your reckless, aggressive attempt to advance has caused arguments and friction to arise. You may be punished or dismissed because of your actions, and as a result, you will experience misfortune. Make what amends you can, and return to your former polite, agreeable manner. There is also an indication that you do not have the requisite strength to advance at this time, or there is someone who is restraining you. In either case, you should not try to obtain your goal at this time.

LINE 4: You are strong and in a position of trust. The situation calls for you to move forward, but doing so may entail a dangerous confrontation with a powerful person. There is danger in the confrontation. This situation calls for great care and caution, but, if you proceed carefully, you will find good fortune. Friendly, good-natured, polite conduct will benefit you greatly. Hold your goal firmly in your mind, remain perservering but cautious, and you will achieve your goal.

LINE 5: You are very strong and in a position of leadership. Remain modest as you move forward because you lack the support of your subordinates, and that is dangerous. However, because you have good intentions and your motives are ethical and honest, you should not be afraid to advance with confidence, but keep the potential danger in mind. Maintain your friendly, agreeable manner and always conduct yourself as a modest, principled, and honorable person. That conduct is sure to meet with success.

TOP LINE: You are nearing your goal. Take some time to look back over your conduct to decide what remains to be accomplished and how to do it. This backward look is essential at this time. Everything flows from what came before, so if your actions are based on what was right and just, supreme good fortune will surely be yours. When you look back, if you find any changes that need to be made to your situation or character, make them, and then move forward confidently to the completion of your goal.

11
T'AI

Peaceful Prosperity, Harmony, Heaven on Earth

THE KUA

This kua is formed of the lower trigram of Heaven, whose motion is upward, and the upper trigram of Earth, whose motion is downward. The two come together to form the condition of Heaven on Earth.

What a wonderful time of perfect harmony this is! The light force is in the ascendancy, and the dark force is diminishing. People in high places are considerate of their subordinates, subordinates are helpful and respectful to those in power, feuds end, friendships are renewed, peace prevails, and pettiness ends. People act from their higher natures rather than from their lower. There is perfect correspondence in all areas, meaning that everyone is at peace with everyone else. This is a time of good fortune and success, when even your small efforts will bring great rewards. This time can be lengthened if conflicts are resolved and you make an extra effort to get along with others by being as courteous and considerate as you can. In this way, all can share in the blessings of this time.

Savor what it feels like when everything goes right, when conflict disappears, when your plans are easily fulfilled, and when your goals are attained almost effortlessly. In such a time of peaceful harmony, it is easy to end long-standing arguments, resolve difficult situations, and bring about peace. Be reverent and grateful for this magical time of peace, and do all you can to make it last as long as possible.

THE LINES

BOTTOM LINE: The time of harmony and prosperity is just beginning. You have the strength to begin moving toward success, and you can draw other strong people along with you. To begin a project at this time will bring good fortune. Take any action you can to encourage and promote this time of peaceful prosperity. Because this is a time when small efforts bring large rewards, any effort that you make now to resolve conflicts, heal broken friendships, and promote peace in your life and the lives of those around you will be greatly rewarded.

LINE 2: You are strong and in a central position. This line advises you to make the most of this time of peaceful prosperity by being tolerant of those who seem less than perfect, overlooking their mistakes, forgiving even intentional violations and offenses, avoiding arguments, and by not forming or taking part in cliques. Develop a strong resolve to finish your projects, and do not neglect even distant or minor concerns. This line also cautions you against showing favoritism and urges you to avoid extremes and to walk "the middle path," where everything you do will benefit you. Use your strength and position to create peace and harmony in all aspects of your life and in the lives of those around you. Your efforts will bring you abundant rewards.

LINE 3: Universal law provides that all times of prosperity shall, at the moment they reach their maximum potential, turn toward a time of decline. Such times of decline are dangerous because they can take away all you have gained, and more. Therefore, in this time of Heaven on Earth, there are certain things you can do to prolong this time of peace, good fortune, and abundance: tolerate those who seem less than perfect, overlook their mistakes, forgive intentional insults, avoid arguments, and do not form or take part in cliques. Develop a strong resolve to finish your projects, and do not neglect even distant or minor concerns while keeping aware of the good fortune you still possess. As long as you are inwardly stronger than your outward circumstances, good fortune will not desert you.

LINE 4: You are in need of help because you lack the resources or the strength to advance on your own. Fortunately, in times of peaceful prosperity such as this, those who are below come to the assistance of those who are above, and you can expect help from your friends, associates, neighbors, and subordinates. Because you are completely sincere and modest, all goes well.

This is also a time when it will benefit you to share your abundance. It is always beneficial to distribute a portion of the prosperity that comes to you as you are accumulating it so that your time of fullness does not turn to emptiness. Avoid joining forces with anyone who seems untrustworthy, even if it appears that such an alliance might bring you something of value. Maintain your grateful, reverent attitude toward All-That-Is.

LINE 5: At this time, you are powerful and in an excellent position to fulfill your dreams and achieve your goals. You have both the power and the complete support and aid of your loyal followers. Moving ahead now will bring success, particularly if you can form an alliance with another, even if he or she is a subordinate.

The guidance is that we should ignore the given social order when we can achieve a greater good by doing so. Entering into a successful union of any kind brings blessings and supreme good fortune. Act so that everything you do is in harmony with this time of peaceful prosperity, and supreme good fortune will be yours.

TOP LINE: The time of peaceful prosperity is about to end. Alert those who are closest to you of the coming decline, and advise them to prepare for it. Helping those close to you in that way will safeguard what you and they have. Do not forcibly resist those who are bringing about the change. Instead, seek to cooperate with them.

Resistance will lead only to embarrassment, for the onset of the decline is due not so much to their efforts as to the inherent Universal law that everything, when it reaches its maximum potential, must turn toward its opposite. Be grateful for the good fortune you still possess. Remain reverent toward the Universe that brought you this time of peaceful prosperity, and know that it has not deserted you. The Universe is already preparing for a new time of prosperity that will come to you after this time passes. In the meantime, remember that you are a golden child of the eternal Universe of which you are an inseparable part. The wisest of sages are content and happy in a time of decline because they know that a time of increase will surely follow.

1 2
P'I

Separation,
Decline

THE KUA

Inferior, unethical people are in power and superior people of honor are retreating, which leads to a state of decline. There is little communication between the two groups. You should rely on your integrity and strong ethical values to see you through this time of decline. Do not be tempted into joining with inferior people despite promises of rewards and riches to come. We sometimes find ourselves associating with unethical people when trying to achieve a common goal, but these alliances may expose us to situations and activities that violate our principles. Taking part in such inappropriate actions will certainly lead to misfortune and remorse. Just as you should not allow yourself to be swept along by unfavorable circumstances, neither should you let unprincipled people corrupt you. If you continue to do what you know to be right, you will overcome even the greatest adversities and temptations, and success and good fortune are sure to be yours.

To protect what you have in this time of decline, you must guard your integrity and honor and distance yourself from unethical people. Remember, this time will pass, and then you will be able to resume working toward fulfilling your plans.

THE LINES

BOTTOM LINE: You are without much power in this time of separation, decline, and standstill. You are surrounded by unethical people who exert a negative influence on everyone whose lives they touch. Fortunately, you have the friendship of an honorable person who is also in a position of authority. By steadfastly closing your mind to the influence of unprincipled, inferior people and following your inclination to adopt your friend's values, you will slowly but surely achieve success.

The time of decline is only just beginning, so you must cultivate enough strength and patience to see you safely through to the end of this period. Above all, continue to act ethically and honorably. If you do, you will protect yourself, and you will be ready to advance after this time of decline comes to an end.

LINE 2: You are in a position of some authority but are surrounded by inferior people. Fortunately, you have the friendship of a person of influence. Look to him or her for help and guidance. Remain true to your gentle nature and to your highest values, turn away from any temptation to violate them in word or deed, and success will be yours in the end. During this time of decline, do not try to win over inferior people by pretending that you share their values. That will only hurt you in the long run. Instead, guard your integrity, and you will see that success and good fortune follow.

LINE 3: You are seeking to attain or have attained a position or goal in a dishonorable manner; shame and disgrace will result. Seek advice from a person in authority with whom you feel a bond, and ask how you can make amends. Reflect on yourself and your conduct, and see where you can do better. If you are to achieve the support of the Universe, you must act with complete integrity and honor. Any action that is not motivated by the intention to be the best person you can will end in failure and disgrace. At this time, you have an opportunity to take a great step toward reaching your goal if you renew your determination to act as a person of integrity and honor. If you do, good fortune will come to you, but, if you do not, you will fall into the pit of failure and humiliation.

LINE 4: You are in a position to end the time of decline. To do so, you will have to follow either the advice of a person in authority or your awareness of what is best and highest within you. Reflect on yourself, your plans, your goals, and on those close to you to see if you can make any changes that will promote this time of renewal. Be reverent and grateful that this time has come, for it is a gift from the Universe that will allow you to begin the upward spiral of your success.

LINE 5: You are in a position of leadership that will enable you to end the decline and turn the situation into a time of increase. To do so, you must be sure to maintain constant vigilance so that matters do not regress. Be on your guard, for, although the time of decline is weakening and giving way to the new time, it is still present. Make every effort to act with honor and integrity as well as instilling those attributes in your associates, for those will be the keys to your success. If you act in accord with what is highest and best within you, you will experience good fortune.

TOP LINE: The time of decline is at an end. You will regain whatever losses you have experienced, provided you have acted and continue to act with integrity and honor. You are in a position to turn the situation into one of great prosperity and joy, but that will require acting with great effort and imagination, coupled with honor and goodness.

13
T'UNG JÊN

Socializing

THE KUA

This is a time when you should go out and spend time socializing with other people. Take every opportunity to do so, for your success depends on it. This time is important because you will be making new contacts, forming new friendships, and creating new alliances. You will benefit if you join with or organize others and then undertake some great endeavor with them. Some of the people you meet may present you with opportunities, or you will perceive opportunities yourself. When that happens, inquire of the oracle again about how to proceed to bring about the best outcome. Not all opportunities are beneficial, so also ask the oracle what you can expect if you act on the particular opportunity. In any event, you must conduct yourself honorably and with the greatest integrity, and you must always act in the best interests of the group. If you are modest and avoid arrogance, people will feel comfortable approaching you. Proceeding in that manner will bring you great success and good fortune. You will also benefit from cultivating good manners and social skills. Because this is the time of socializing, you may go forth confidently, knowing that you will be received with friendliness and goodwill and that success will come to you.

THE LINES

BOTTOM LINE: It is time for you to go out and meet with existing and former friends as well as making new acquaintances. To do so will bring success because this is the time of socializing. By acting in accord with this time, you will make new friends and discover new opportunities. Be confident and be true to your principles. Do not let fear stand in your way because you have the backing of the Universe in your social endeavors. You have the strength and charisma to achieve your goals, and you will reach them without anyone resenting you or holding anything against you. The keys to your success are modesty, friendliness, and integrity. Those attributes will bring good fortune.

LINE 2: This line indicates that you are limiting your social activities to your immediate circle. That will not work to your benefit. You must expand the scope of your activities by taking part in different gatherings, seeking out new friends, and adding new and different types of activities to your days. Be outgoing, friendly, modest, and honorable, and you will enjoy good rewards.

LINE 3: You are aggressively seeking one or more people with whom you can socialize or align yourself, but your motives seem devious. Examine yourself to see if you are being the best person you can be. Reflect on whether you are truly acting with integrity and honor. You may have hidden agendas or motives that are unworthy of an honorable person. If so, you will fail to achieve the union you seek. Only if you act out of the highest principles and motives will you achieve your goal and enjoy success. Because of your mixed motives, you may experience a long period during which your social activities will not result in the ties you are seeking. You can shorten that time by avoiding any underhanded behavior and remaining true to the highest ideals and most ethical conduct.

LINE 4: Your strength has led you to act too forcefully and too aggressively. Now is a time for you to rely on your good sense and call a halt to any aggressive attitudes or activities. Instead, you must be low-key and accommodating if you are to achieve your goal. By toning down how you present yourself and eliminating any aggressiveness, you will find good fortune.

LINE 5: You have great strength and are in a position of leadership. You wish to socialize, mingle, or join with a person but are being blocked. That person also feels as you do and would like to join forces with you, but first there are issues that still have to be worked out. You may feel disappointed, but if you remain courageous and persevering, you will eventually overcome all obstacles and you will achieve the alliance you seek. When the alliance has been achieved, you will have much cause for rejoicing. To achieve your goal, it is essential that you remain modest and ethical. Avoid any underhanded thoughts or motives. By acting with integrity, you will find what you seek.

TOP LINE: You wish to socialize and mingle freely and openly with a person or group of your choice but are facing obstacles that are too great to be overcome completely. However, you have accomplished part of your goal in that you are able to spend time with these people occasionally, even if in out-of-the-way places. Do not blame yourself for failing to meet your goal of socializing freely with those of your choice. Instead, be grateful for what you have achieved. Continue to act modestly and honorably and avoid feelings of hostility toward those who are blocking you. Other opportunities lie ahead that will bring you success and good fortune.

14
TA YU

Great Abundance,
Great Wealth

THE KUA

This is the kua of abundance that has already been accumulated as it relates to the topic of your question. With abundance comes responsibility. To enjoy abundance, you must be a good caretaker of it. You must act modestly and not selfishly. Do not withhold all you have accumulated. In addition to the abundance you already enjoy, you will have the opportunity to gain more, but for that to happen requires that you act in accord with what is highest and best within you and that you work to reach new heights of honor and integrity. By eliminating bad influences from your life and encouraging good ones, you will live in accord with the highest Universal principles, which bring supreme success because of the fulfillment of natural law. Many opportunities for advancement and gain will now come your way, but even the greatest opportunity will come to nothing if you do not handle it properly. If you have the opportunity to help an influential or highly placed friend, associate, or person, do so, for that will bring you great good fortune. To be a good caretaker of the abundance that has already come to you, be mindful of your conduct, remain modest, continue to behave with honor and integrity, share some of your abundance as you accumulate it, and counsel others when the opportunity presents itself. In this way, you will enjoy long-lasting success and good fortune.

THE LINES

BOTTOM LINE: You are strong and in a position suited to your circumstances. Avoid forming relationships with unethical or underhanded people. Keep in mind how hard it is to administer great abundance properly, for nothing is easier than to become vain or overbold when such abundance comes. Also, great abundance is dangerous because others may seek to take it from you. Be cautious in your dealings and beware of those who want your abundance for themselves. Be a good caretaker of your abundance, and you will continue to have success.

LINE 2: You are strong and in a position of influence. Also, a wise and gentle person in authority is on your side. You can rely on that person for help. You may see the need to transport or move a portion of your abundance. You may undertake the move successfully. There is an indication that the time has come for you to take a major step forward in your spiritual growth. To do so will bring you great benefit and will result in your accumulating important spiritual wisdom. Remember that teaching is a holy task and that you should share your wisdom, because teaching should be withheld from no one. It will benefit you to undertake a project at this time.

LINE 3: You have an opportunity to offer help to a person in an influential position. Perhaps a portion of your assets will fill a great need. Only a generous-minded person is capable of going to someone in authority and making such an offer, for petty people do not think that way and cannot take such action. You will be well rewarded for this timely and appropriate offer. However, be sure that you are motivated by a sincere desire to help, for, if you act purely to obtain some benefit for yourself, it will work against you. If you are sincerely helpful, you will see your star rise high and shine brightly.

LINE 4: You are strong and in a high, trusted position. Although you have close relationships with a powerful person and with other wealthy, influential people, you must avoid becoming confused about their possessions and yours, their fame and yours, their duties and yours, and their position and yours. What is theirs belongs to them, not to you. Avoid taking credit for their accomplishments, their wealth, or their position. Nor should you make any attempt to gain a share of their wealth in an underhanded fashion, for that will work powerfully against you. Remain loyal and modest, do as much good as you can, and work to benefit those in power. Then, no one will reproach you or criticize your actions, and you will enjoy success and good fortune. You will also see yourself rise quickly through the ranks.

LINE 5: You have attained a position of leadership and have amassed great abundance while remaining modest and unselfish. For these reasons, others respect and like you, and your followers find you easy to deal with. You do not take advantage of others, your sincerity is your hallmark, and you maintain excellent relationships with your allies and followers. By continuing to conduct yourself in a dignified manner and by keeping your wisdom simple, you will enjoy further good fortune.

TOP LINE: Even though you have achieved the pinnacle of abundance and success, you still continue to behave appropriately, with modesty and dignity. Therefore, anything you undertake will succeed because your actions are in accord with Universal law. Good fortune and the blessings of Heaven are yours. As the great Chinese sage Confucius said twenty-five hundred years ago, "To bless means to help." When Heaven blesses you, it helps you, and to be helped by Heaven is to be helped indeed!

1 5
CH'IEN

Modesty, Humbleness, Moderation

THE KUA

The course of action you are considering at this time will achieve a modest success. Be content with that, for, once it has come to you, any further effort to push it to greater heights will turn it into failure. This kua advises you not to brag, complain about your problems, or strive beyond your capabilities. Always reduce what is too much and add to what is too little. As a result, you will enjoy continued success and good fortune because the Universe always favors the modest and undermines the arrogant. Those who boast of their power, wealth, position, promotions, successes, or influential friends inevitably invite misfortune and humiliation. Boasting reveals only that you feel inferior, inadequate, and insecure, and that you are trying to inflate your own importance. Principled people believe who they are and what they have are enough, and they let those qualities or possessions speak for themselves. Such people always act modestly and thus assure their continued success.

This kua advises you to keep your goals modest and realistic. Otherwise, the small success possible for you at this time will turn into failure. If you attempt too much, you will end by succeeding in nothing.

Keep in mind that, if you share the credit for your successes with others, your area of influence will grow. This is the kua of moderation, so avoid taking any extreme actions, for they will not benefit you. Walk the middle road to your success. Avoid extremes.

The ancient Chinese sages valued modesty and moderation above all other qualities of character and behavior. If you make boastful claims at the outset of a project, you will find it far more difficult to attain your goal successfully. If, on the other hand, you avoid extravagant claims or predictions, no resistance will arise against you.

Cultivate modesty, and your progress will be swift and sure because no one will feel resentment toward you. If you remain modest in spite of your merits and achievements, others will love and respect you, and you will win the support necessary to carry out even difficult and dangerous undertakings. If you make boastful claims, and then achieve only a moderate success that still falls short of your claims, people will say that you have failed. Remember, the Universe helps the modest to prosper but brings down the arrogant.

THE LINES

BOTTOM LINE: Your situation at this time calls for an extra measure of modesty. Goals are always more easily attained if no great claims are made beforehand, for then neither resentment nor resistance will arise against you. Humility creates good fortune, so that even difficult and dangerous undertakings succeed. This line cautions you that, because you are just starting out, you should not set your goal so high that you cannot reach it. However, if you remain modest in your attitude and in setting your goals, you will achieve success. It is better to achieve a small success rather than attempting too much and failing.

LINE 2: Because you are close to a person of influence and authority, it is essential that you cultivate the utmost modesty in both your speech and your demeanor. Your words should spring from your heart and should display the sincerity of your intentions. That will bring you success and honor, and others will not resent you. Those who are modest are never passed over when the time for advancement is at hand.

LINE 3: If you work hard and persevere, you will achieve your goal and earn great recognition. You face danger in that it is difficult to remain humble in the face of acclaim, but that is essential to your continued success. If you remain modest, you will attract followers who are happy to work with you. Confucius said, "When a man does not boast of his efforts and achievements and does not count his merits a virtue, he is a man of great understanding and worth; for all his merits, he does not put on airs and is willing to be in a subordinate position. Noble of nature and reverent in his conduct, the modest man is therefore able to succeed."

Persevere until you reach your goal, and you will have good fortune and success. Remember to share the credit with others.

LINE 4: You are in a dangerous position close to a person in authority. Do not attempt to block or hinder that person. Instead, seek to assist him or her. If you remain modest, carry out your duties faithfully, show respect toward those in authority at all times, and cooperate with your subordinates, all will be well. The danger will pass you by, and you will have good fortune.

LINE 5: You are in a position of leadership. Do not boast of your position, achievements, or possessions. If you do, you will alienate your friends, neighbors, and associates. In your position as a leader, you may find that you must use forceful measures to achieve either obedience from those whom you lead or to enforce order in your sphere of authority. If you do not attempt too much and are content with your modest achievements, you will have good fortune and long-lasting success.

TOP LINE: You have become too easygoing, and now you must take forceful measures to reestablish order and your authority within the sphere that you govern. Because your intentions are honorable and based on what you believe to be just and right, all will be well, provided you remain modest and use only enough force to reestablish order. You may also find that you must use your strength and that of your associates to achieve unity with another or to attain a goal. Do not be too forceful, or you will turn your success into failure.

16
YÜ

Enthusiasm, Revelry, Celebration

THE KUA

This kua takes its meaning from its two trigrams, Chen (thunder) over K'un (Earth). Thunder resounding powerfully over the Earth symbolizes great enthusiasm, revelry, and celebration. In such times, you will find it easy to enlist helpers and to set them to work.

You will do well to create enthusiasm in them because it will unify them, strengthen their commitment, and fill them with the energy and good spirits needed to reach great goals. You can generate enthusiasm by setting clear-cut and worthwhile goals that will inspire them. At this time, your efforts have been or will be highly successful. Be confident about the outcome of your plans. During this time of enthusiasm, you may anticipate success in undertaking even difficult goals. After you achieve your success, however, be restrained in your celebrations so you do not misuse your energy and stir up resentment or criticism from others.

THE LINES

BOTTOM LINE: You are at the beginning, so it is too soon to celebrate. If you do, misfortune will result. Be cautious and do not boast about your ties with well-known people. Such behavior will only cause others to resent and resist you. When you boast, you prove only that you feel inferior and are trying to inflate your worth and importance. Because your own position is weak, such actions are out of place and will produce unfortunate results.

Still, this is the kua of enthusiasm, so it is appropriate to feel enthusiastic about your plans and prospects, but do not let this show too openly except for those who are part of your plan.

LINE 2: It is too early to celebrate. Even if you see others celebrating, do not let yourself become overexcited, for their revelry will be short-lived. If you see a need to withdraw or retreat, act swiftly, and good fortune will follow.

LINE 3: You have an opportunity to advance now or in the immediate future. You must perceive the right moment for action and take it, so that your opportunity is not lost. Be on the lookout because if you wait too long, you will miss your chance, and what would have been easy becomes difficult.

LINE 4: This is your time to be the inspiration for celebration and enthusiasm for those around you. You are the strong person in the group, so you easily attract helpers. Cast aside any doubts about your abilities or actions. You will accomplish great deeds, and your success is assured. Remember that enthusiasm is the essential ingredient to your success. Encourage others and set meaningful goals that will arouse your helpers' enthusiasm, so that they can commit themselves to them wholeheartedly.

LINE 5: You are in a place of authority, but someone else may be the center of attention. Your envy of his or her popularity is dulling your enthusiasm and may even be making you feel upset. Such feelings are unworthy of you and will only cause you harm if you let them continue. Because you are in authority, it will be to your benefit to fulfill your duties as well as you can. If you refuse to give way to excessive enthusiasm and do all you can to further your plans or those of the group, all will be well.

TOP LINE: Do not indulge in excessive revelry or celebration, for it is unsuitable to your position and you are running the risk of misfortune if you persist. People are looking to you for guidance. If you display excessive exuberance, it will send them the wrong message. You can achieve success and good fortune, but only if you pull back immediately and become serious and disciplined.

1 7
SUI

Leading and Following

THE KUA

This is the time for you to be joyous and enthusiastic, which will attract followers. Cultivating a warm, engaging, helpful attitude will win their deepest affection and even their love. You have received this kua because you have attracted the notice of a person or group with whom or with which you wish to establish a close relationship. If you continue to be enthusiastic, sincere, and thoughtful, the relationship will blossom. Because this is a time of following as well as leading, it is appropriate that you seek and follow the advice or guidance of another, even though he or she may be in a subordinate position. If you wish to rule, you must first learn to serve. Only in that way will you come to understand those who will eventually serve you. Because you understand them and their duties, you will not ask more of them than they can give, and you will know how to inspire them with enthusiasm and loyalty.

The only valid reason why you should want to rule is so you can better serve your followers. Unprincipled people seek to rule so they can wield power over and control others, but this leads to their downfall. If you are unprepared or unwilling to serve your followers, it is better for them and for you that you never become their leader, because, if you do, and then cease to serve them, they will abandon you. All your efforts will have been for naught, and you will suffer great humiliation. Only through serving your followers can you obtain from them the wholehearted assent necessary if they are to follow you. If you continue to follow the path of the superior person and to persevere in what is good, right, fair, and just, you will enjoy great benefits, and no one will resent or resist you. Because of the effort that this time of leading and following requires, be sure to rest, relax, and nourish yourself properly. Rest and activity must follow each other in proper order if you are to be successful at this time. Also, it is essential that you remain modest and share the credit for any goals you achieve. This kua foretells supreme success.

THE LINES

BOTTOM LINE: A change in goals, plans, policies, or methods of operation may present itself. Persevering in making that change will bring good fortune. Seek advice about what changes to make and how to accomplish them from an associate, friend, or acquaintance, even if that person is in a subordinate position. Go out and mingle freely with friends and foes alike.

Few people even think about mingling with their adversaries, much less actually doing so. If you do, however, you will expand your point of view, learn about new ideas that you can consider, and perhaps even find a middle ground that will end the hostility between you. By enthusiastically attracting followers and friends, you will achieve great merit, reach your goals easily, and enjoy good fortune.

LINE 2: This line counsels you to make a careful choice about the people with whom you surround yourself. Look for people who have your best interests at heart. Your friends should be strong, good natured, well intentioned, light giving, enthusiastic, right thinking, moral, ethical, honest, responsible and rooted in achieving something good for the whole of the people. To the extent that you allow yourself to associate with people who are unworthy, poor mannered, evil minded, cruel, and of low moral and ethical character, you give up your own dignity and lose connections with people of better quality. If you sever your ties with people of poor character and keep your friends who are of good character, you will have good fortune.

LINE 3: You are associating with people of high moral values and good ethical standards. Those associations will bring you good fortune. You also have been associating with people of low moral and ethical values. This is a time to cut your ties with those people. You may feel a sense of loss, but it is necessary to sever your ties with those people if you are to achieve your goal. Your cutting of those ties may cause them to gossip about you, but they cannot hurt you in any way. This is a wonderful time because it means that you are outgrowing your old ways and developing a much higher standard of behavior.

LINE 4: You are strong and occupy a strong area of influence. You should be careful about choosing your friends, associates, and helpers. People who flatter you simply to gain some sort of advantage for themselves are of little use to you. Do not let them cloud your good judgment when choosing the right people for the group.

LINE 5: You are strong and in a position of leadership with the support of your followers. If you are sincere and cultivate high moral and ethical values, you will have success and will bring about good fortune for all. You will benefit by defining the type of person you want to be and let that be your guiding light. Once you have defined the type of person that you want to be, make sure all your actions are based on achieving that goal. To remain at the height of your powers, if you have not already done so, read the section called "The Superior Person" on page 387 and make those characteristics your own.

TOP LINE: You are a wise and gentle person who commands great respect because of your strict adherence to the highest principles. Although you have set yourself apart from your associates, one of them may need your help, which you should agree to give, even though it puts you under an obligation that you might not want. However, because you are good and honorable and willing to teach those less experienced than yourself, you will be supported even in the spiritual realm. That is indeed a great blessing.

1 8
KU

Correcting Deficiencies

THE KUA

At this time, there is a great opportunity to take a major step forward. There is a deficiency in your situation that will be greatly to your advantage to correct. The deficiency may be psychological, having to do with beliefs you are holding that are not in accord with the truth of the situation, or it may be that some aspect of your external life requires improvement. The deficiency may include your physical health, your work, your love relationship, your business relationships and related business matters, your spiritual well-being, financial matters, or undertakings of any nature. The deficiencies most likely exist in the situation surrounding your question.

Regarding psychological deficiencies, throughout your life until now, you have been taught lessons. Some of those lessons may not have been in accord with Universal law or truth. By acting in accord with those lessons, you may have brought misfortune your way. You may also have adopted behavior patterns that are not only not benefiting you, but are creating problems for you. When you begin correcting psychological conditions, asking those who know you well to sincerely tell you what improvements they think you could make will be of great benefit to you. Be open-minded about their suggestions, even though you may feel hurt or offended by what they say.

Clinging to past hurts and injuries is foolish, and is one of the most important inner conditions you can change. What happened is finished, even if it happened only yesterday. We cannot change past events, but we can change how we view them. If you are permitting events from your past to bring you pain today, you are the foolish one who is giving those events their power to hurt you. Whatever the event was, whether it hurt you, took something from you, betrayed you, violated you, or caused you mental or physical pain, it is over. It has no power to hurt you beyond that which you give it—and what you give, you can take away. Because you live in a Universe where everything that happens benefits you, continuing to carry hurts from the past shows that you lack true understanding of your Universe, and alerts you to an important deficiency that you can begin correcting immediately.

The feelings you hold in your mind manifest in your body. It is the nature of the mind to create, and what you hold there will somehow manifest itself in your body. If you hold worry and anxiety in your mind, they will appear in your body as pain, disease, stress, and illness. If you hold gratitude, joy, and reverence in your mind, they will manifest as glowing, radiant health. That you are consulting the I Ching at this time shows that you have already begun learning lessons that are in accord with Universal truth.

If you have a shortcoming that is obvious to you, or if there is an obvious deficiency in your situation, it is serious indeed and requires immediate attention. You must plan carefully if you are to reach your goal. Once you begin taking corrective measures, keep a careful eye on your progress so that regression does not set in. Through constant perseverance in healing the deficiency inherent within yourself or the situation, you will eventually reach your goal.

As the ancient text states, "Before the starting point, three days; after the starting point, three days." This refers to the time you need to spend defining what you need to change, planning the changes, and continuing to be watchful as your plan unfolds. By being diligent in your efforts, and persevering until you reach your goal, you will enjoy supreme success and great good fortune.

THE LINES

BOTTOM LINE: You are just at the beginning, and you will most likely not receive any help. However, you will succeed if you act in accord with the guidance offered above. There is danger in the situation, so caution is required. If you make diligent efforts to find out what needs correcting and to persevere in correcting it, you will have success and good fortune. The ancient text speaks of correcting deficiencies caused by the father. If such is the case for you, the shortcomings you must correct most likely lie in the area of behaviors or ways of proceeding that you learned from him or that were caused by him. Or, you may be continuing to follow traditions that are no longer necessary or appropriate for you.

LINE 2: Whether a shortcoming is an inner or outer condition, you are in a good position to correct it, and it is in your power to do so. However, you must proceed gently and with deliberation. This deficiency has most likely been caused by a lazy attitude or some other character flaw, but you can correct it if you take forceful measures and learn to discipline yourself. If deficiencies caused by the mother are an issue, these are most likely due to behaviors or ways of proceeding that you learned from her or that were caused by her. Or, you may be continuing to follow traditions that are no longer necessary or appropriate for you.

LINE 3: In correcting your shortcomings, be careful not to use too much force. This is a situation in which gentleness will produce better results than pushing too hard. At this time, you have already begun the work of correcting your deficiencies but have acted too drastically or forcefully. Because of this, you will feel regret; however, no great blame attaches to your progress and good fortune will prevail in the end because of the measures you have taken to improve yourself. If limitations caused by the father are the issue, these mostly likely lie in the area of behaviors or ways of proceeding that you learned from or that were caused by him. Or, you may be continuing to follow traditions that are no longer necessary or appropriate for you.

LINE 4: You are aware of your failings, but you are not taking the necessary actions to correct them. To continue on like that will bring humiliation. Do an inventory of yourself, see what needs to be corrected and attend to it. There is an indication that you may not be equal to the task because the problems are so deeply rooted. If that is the case, seek the help of someone who is qualified to help you overcome your problem. If setting right what was spoiled by the father is the issue, it most likely lies in the behaviors that you learned from or that were caused by him. Or, you may be continuing to follow traditions that are no longer necessary or appropriate for you.

LINE 5: You are in an excellent position to make the corrections necessary, but you are not strong enough to do it on your own. Enlist the aid of your helpers or friends in helping you to make the necessary corrections, Correcting the problems will bring you honor and will lead to good fortune and recognition. If setting right what was spoiled by the father is the issue, it most likely lies in the area of behaviors or ways of proceeding that you learned from him or that were caused by him. Or, you may be continuing to follow traditions that are no longer necessary or appropriate for you.

TOP LINE: Even though highly placed people may ask you to correct the deficiencies inherent in the situation, you must abstain from taking part in the corrective action. Instead, pay attention to yourself and to your own affairs or attend to much loftier goals that you set for yourself.

19
LIN

Advancing, Progress

THE KUA

This is a fortunate time when your advances will be crowned with supreme success. You must make the best use of this time of rapid, easy advance by acting with great determination and perseverance, for it will not last forever. The ancient text states that you should be untiring in your leadership and teaching and unlimited in your patience, tolerance, and protection of people. To be tolerant, means to overlook others' faults and mistakes. Overlook even intentional transgressions, for that will prevent arguments and ensure your continued success. During this time of rapid advance, be tireless in bringing your plans to completion. This is the time for action. Do not be fearful, for your success is certain. If you see a problem coming, you can neutralize it before it grows strong. However, if the setback does occur, do not be dismayed. In the end, it will work to your complete benefit, particularly if you act as if the only reason it has occurred was so that you could benefit.

THE LINES

BOTTOM LINE: You are just beginning to be able to make an advance. You have the necessary strength to do so, but you will find it to your benefit if you join with someone or some group. Be careful not to let the interests of the group sweep you away if they are not in accord with your highest good. By persevering in an honorable course of action, you will have good fortune.

LINE 2: You are strong and have advanced to a key position. By finding someone with whom you can join forces or by joining a group, you will make greater advances than you can alone. Joining and advancing will bring you good fortune, and everything that occurs will benefit you. By acting in accord with all that is highest and best within yourself, you will see your plans come to fruition. If you act honorably and according to the principles of the superior person, you will travel the paths of life swiftly, honestly, and courageously, and you will find good fortune.

LINE 3: You have advanced to the point of having achieved some power and influence. Those achievements have created within you a feeling of relaxed contentment. Those feelings will fail to benefit you if they cause you to become careless and too easygoing. If you go on in that way, misfortune will result. However, if you become aware of those attitudes and their consequences and correct them, you will free yourself of blame, and good fortune will come to you.

LINE 4: You have advanced to a strong position of influence but have remained modest, cooperative, and helpful to your subordinates. Maintaining your modest attitude while using your influence to help a subordinate to advance will serve you well. Not only will no one resent you for your efforts, but you will also be well rewarded for providing such assistance.

LINE 5: You have advanced to a position of leadership and are at the height of your powers, yet have remained modest and helpful to all. To maintain this high standing, you must use your wisdom and position to attract loyal followers and to help your present followers. Wise leaders are known by the people with whom they surround themselves. Once you find good people to help you, allow them the freedom to make decisions and to act on them. That is the correct action for you and will lead to good fortune.

TOP LINE: In the ancient text, this line refers to a great sage who has stepped outside the affairs of the world but who returns to teach the people in their time of need. As it relates to you, it means that you have become a wise and knowledgeable person, and that you should now turn your attention to helping others with your wisdom, influence, and knowledge. The people you teach will be greatly benefited by your wisdom. Your great-heartedness will bring you good fortune.

20
KUAN

Looking Inward, Seeing the World Outwardly, Being Looked Up To as an Example

THE KUA

This kua takes its meaning from its visual resemblance to a tall tower. The four lower broken lines represent the legs, and the top two solid lines represent the platform. Standing on this tower, one can see far away and be seen from far away, which gives rise to the meaning of this kua, "Being Looked Up To as an Example." The upper trigram, which symbolizes the gentle wind that blows over the earth and penetrates everywhere, suggests that inner and outer seeing should miss nothing. You are in a position to set a good example for others by the values you hold and the beneficial actions you take. When you act in accordance with Universal laws and what is highest and best within you, others will see clearly that your actions are in harmony with All-That-Is, and they will look up to you as a role model. They will also see you as a person worthy of loyalty and of being followed even into dangerous and difficult undertakings such as those indicated in the ancient phrase, "crossing the great water." This is an opportunity for you to look inward to see whether you are fearless, brave, greathearted, loyal, kind, dedicated, consistent, honorable, gentle, and open-handed, or whether you are harboring any weak, unworthy, or selfish tendencies. This is an extraordinary time for you, for you can make great advances inwardly and outwardly, and you will find it easy to gather loyal followers.

THE LINES

BOTTOM LINE: A worthy and learned person from whom you could learn may be at hand, but you are failing to recognize him or her as such. Seek out that person and ask for guidance. There is an indication that your outlook is too narrow, and it will be to your advantage to expand it by seeking the counsel of that worthy and learned person. You will also benefit greatly from studying the two volumes of *I Ching Wisdom* (Power Press), and other great books of wisdom such as *I Ching Life* (Power Press).

LINE 2: You have a good relationship with people in positions of power who can assist you greatly, but you are failing to pay them proper respect. You are thinking only of yourself, and that narrow way of thinking and acting is shameful and will lead to misfortune. Expand your view of the world beyond yourself and your situation. Become aware of the bigger picture. Look around and see who can assist you, but be respectful and humble. If you ask for help, you will receive it, and you will benefit greatly.

LINE 3: This is a time for you to look inward and reflect deeply on what you have accomplished, on how you have affected others, and on who you truly are. The paths of inferior people are filled with pitfalls of their own making. The paths of superior people are filled with the accomplishments of their own making. If your self-examination shows you to be worthy, your advance will be successful. If not, you should retreat and take time to improve yourself. If you have not already done so, it will benefit you to study the section on "The Superior Person"(page 387). Only through daily self-renewal of your character will you remain at the height of your powers.

LINE 4: You are in an excellent position to be of service to your superiors or to your cause. Study the existing conditions, and use your influence to bring about a period of prosperity and peace. Acting in this manner will result in good fortune and success for all concerned. If you cannot do this, perhaps you can trust another with that undertaking. If you do, give that person full authority to act on your behalf or on behalf of those in power.

LINE 5: You are in a position of leadership, and everyone is looking up to you. If you are to remain at the height of your powers, you must examine yourself and the results of your actions to see how you can improve yourself and better serve the people. Only thorough and fearless self-examination will give you the clarity to see whether you need to make improvements. If you are careful and diligent in that self-examination and make whatever beneficial changes you can, you will have good fortune.

TOP LINE: This is a time for you to take an objective look back on your life and to learn from it. Do not become preoccupied with unattained goals or frustrated hopes; they are of no concern. What is important is the backward look you take, for it will reveal to you what the future may hold. Be patient. You have an eternity of lifetimes ahead of you in which to carry out your work.

21
SHIH HO

Corrective Punishment

THE KUA

This kua depicts being punished and punishing others. Punishment should never be an end in itself, nor carried out to deliberately hurt another, but should be used only to guide someone back onto the path of correct behavior, what the ancient text refers to as "the path of the superior person."

Corrective punishment becomes necessary when we deviate from the path of abundant life, for the pitfalls we then experience will motivate us to return to the correct path. It is always beneficial to administer justice, which brings success. The best way to deter both wrongdoers and criminals is to make the law clear, and punishment swift and certain.

In the Universe, there is no lag time. Every action produces a result, and the result is always in exact accord with the action. No one can escape the corrective measures of the Universe, but remember, these measures are only for the benefit of the one who receives it. If you have received this kua, either you need and will receive corrective punishment, or another person needs it and you will provide it. Take heart, because corrective punishment is always for the complete benefit of the person on whom it is imposed, whether you or someone else.

THE LINES

BOTTOM LINE: A first offender or a young offender requires corrective punishment. Because he or she is potentially a strong and good person, no one will blame you for being lenient, provided the punishment is sufficient to deter the offender from committing future offenses. This situation requires good judgment, because too much severity can turn a mere wrongdoer into a hardened criminal. Receiving this line as part of your answer may mean that you are the person who needs corrective punishment. If so, and it is administered to you, remember that it is for your complete benefit and for the sole purpose of causing you to recognize that you have strayed from the path of abundant life. If you accept the punishment with that benefit in mind, or if you administer corrective punishment to another with that in mind, good fortune will result.

LINE 2: This kua indicates that you or someone else has become a callous and unrepentant wrongdoer or criminal who requires punishment to prevent further offenses. In this situation, if you are the one who is doing the punishing, more is better than less because if the punishment is inadequate, the offenses are likely to be repeated.

LINE 3: The person who requires corrective punishment is a strong, callous offender. Although you lack the strength and the authority to carry out the required punishment, you are still required to do so. The situation poses some danger in that the offender will spread lies and spiteful rumors about you. This may cause you some embarrassment, but no one will hold anything against you, and, in the end, all will go well. Do everything you can to follow the guidance of this line, and, even if you fall short of completing the punishment, consider that you fulfilled your obligation. You will have done all that was possible, and you will receive no blame for your actions.

LINE 4: Both the case in question and the corrective punishment to be administered are difficult. The issues are not entirely clear, and the offender is strong and perhaps callous. Although you are strong enough to carry out your obligation, your position is weak and danger is present. By holding steadfastly to what is right and by fulfilling your duties, you will gain good fortune.

LINE 5: You are in a strong position to decide the issues, which are clear to you. Still, the task is difficult and dangerous. Someone may try to bribe you, and this is probably the source of the danger you face. Although you are inclined to be lenient, be as firm and steadfast as the situation requires. Above all, keep to the right path. If you do, no one will hold your actions against you.

TOP LINE: You committed numerous offenses and have grown callous, unrepentant, and are unwilling or unable to listen to good advice. Even though you are a strong person, your position is weak, and you are outside the circle of influential people. Your actions have made it impossible for you to avoid misfortune. If, however, you return to the path of the superior person, you may be able to minimize your punishment.

2 2
PI

Outer Refinement

THE KUA

This kua refers to the refinement and enhancement of the external aspects of your life, such as your home, your social situation, your physical appearance, your possessions, your work, your friendships, your relationships, and your situation in general. It is through the refinement of the external aspects of your life that you will achieve your goal.

Remember that the greatest beauty lies in the original form, not in its outer adornments. It is better to let the original form stand forth rather than attempt to beautify it with too much outer adornment. Be patient and persevering in maintaining your decision to refine the outward aspects of your life, and you will achieve your success and achieve that which you desire. By refining the outward aspects of your life, you will be able to succeed in the more controversial and complicated issues that you may have to face. This is a kua of success and indicates that refining the external aspects of your life will greatly benefit you. You will do best if you begin by setting and achieving small goals.

THE LINES

BOTTOM LINE: You are just beginning to refine the external aspects of your life. Highly placed people offer you assistance, but this offer may not be coming from an honorable source, or it may not be proper for you to accept it. Because you are strong enough, know enough, and have the resources to bring about the refinements you desire on your own, it is proper for you to decline the assistance.

LINE 2: Refining and enhancing your external appearance and general living conditions will allow you to associate more freely with those in power and will facilitate your upward progress.

LINE 3: Because you are a strong and intelligent person, you attract the attention of those around you. This enhances your stature in your community or group. If you remain steadfastly modest and unpretentious, and do not let this attention go to your head, good fortune will follow. It will benefit you to improve your general living conditions—a new wardrobe, new furniture, or a new vehicle, or perhaps you should begin an exercise regimen.

LINE 4: You are at an important crossroads in your life. You must decide how you want to live: simply and unpretentiously, or stylishly and elegantly; in the public eye, or quietly and privately. The ancient text indicates that you will be provided with a clue as to which course of action will be of the greatest benefit to you. In making your decision, you will attract the attention of someone who may appear unworthy of trust. However, at the proper time, you will learn that this person has good intentions, and you will form an alliance with him or her.

LINE 5: You find yourself in the company of a person of great refinement who has an elegant lifestyle to which your own does not measure up. This will cause you some embarrassment, and sorrow. Do not be overly concerned; it will all work out in the end.

If you give that person or others a gift, it is the sincerity with which the gift is given and not the price that matters. Avoid trying to bolster or inflate your self-image with boasting or immodesty of any sort, for that will work against you. In the end, because you keep your sincerity, all goes well and you will experience good fortune.

TOP LINE: You have achieved your goals and have refined yourself and your lifestyle to the maximum. Any further attempts at external refinement will only detract from who you are and what you have. Instead, returning to a life of simplicity at this time will bring you good fortune, and no one will look down on you or find fault with you for your actions.

23
PO

Undermining, Overthrowing, Ending a Relationship

THE KUA

Forces have been set in motion that may lead or have led to the ending of a relationship with a person, group, place of employment, or organization. The best course of action, if the relationship is to be ended, is to end it harmoniously, which will prevent it from deteriorating further and will eliminate long-lasting ill will. Because you have received this kua in answer to your question, it means that the possibility of ending some type of relationship exists. If you wish for the relationship to continue, heeding the advice of this kua will help to preserve it. If the relationship in question involves an organization, group, or social structure of any kind, this kua indicates that its leader, who may be yourself, or those in authority are being undermined. Fortunately, you or they are of extraordinary integrity and, being at the top of the kua, still powerful. If you are a member of the undermining force, disassociate yourself from it at once. If you are the person being undermined, conduct yourself with complete honor, integrity, and generosity, for therein lies your strength and influence. You or your cause will benefit greatly if you offer help or assets to those below you. This generosity will help you to maintain your position of influence and power. No matter which of the above conditions are at issue here, you will weather this time of "Undermining, Overthrowing, or Ending a Relationship," provided you are generous with those under you and persevere in fulfilling your duties and fulfilling your goals, and act only out of the purest of motives.

THE LINES

BOTTOM LINE: The undermining people have just begun their movement and will soon have a strong position of influence over the person or group of which you are, or would like to be, a part. Their position will become so powerful that anyone who opposes them will suffer harm. Your best course of action is to keep a low profile and not try to stop the people who are responsible for the undermining. If the issue is a relationship, inferior people will undermine you to the point that you cannot make any progress. The situation bodes disaster. Your best defense is to remain so upright in your character that you are above reproach.

LINE 2: The undermining effort has reached a critical stage, and the forces mounting this sabotage are gaining control. To oppose them openly is to invite disaster. Maintain a low profile. You will receive no backing from anyone above or below you, and you will have to stand alone. Your lack of support places you in a situation that requires extreme caution. Stubbornly maintaining your position or point of view will lead to your downfall, but, if you try to reach a compromise, you may be able to achieve a small gain.

LINE 3: Your allies or associates, who are of weak character, are trying to overthrow the last good and honorable person in a position of influence or authority. Remain in close communication with the person they are trying to overthrow and gain strength and guidance from him or her. If you see an opportunity to support the person who is being undermined, take it. Supporting that person may bring you into conflict with your previous allies, but there is no help for that. In the end, you will be better off supporting those in a position of influence and authority because they represent the light force and are working for a higher good.

LINE 4: Here the undermining forces are so strong that they cannot be warded off. As a result, you experience misfortune. The best you can do is to endure this time until it passes by. You will have the best chance of surviving this time by remaining true to that which is highest and best within you.

LINE 5: You are the leader, and you support the person or cause being undermined. Use your authority to dissuade the undermining forces from their efforts, and encourage them to change their position and support the target of their attack. Your honorable course of action will bring you good fortune. However, if you have been aligned with the undermining forces in any way, break off from them immediately and support the person being undermined.

TOP LINE: Congratulations. By maintaining your integrity and remaining true to your principles, you have survived the undermining forces, which have now been defeated. Great good fortune will result.

24
FU

Return of the Light Force

THE KUA

The forces of light and dark, which represent good and evil, alternate constantly. An increase of one always leads to a decrease of the other. This kua indicates that the time of darkness is past, bringing the victory of the light that is now in the ascendancy. This is a time for you to look inward, to be in touch with the Divine within you, and to perceive your inner light, which is the ascending force of life in nature and in you. To sense that inner light is to experience your oneness with All-That-Is. The return of the light force brings great good fortune. Projects are blessed, relationships prosper, feuds end, friendships are reborn, and people are kinder and more thoughtful to each other. It is a time when people act from their higher natures rather than their lower. It is a time of rejoicing because the return of the light force brings with it the blessings of the Universe. You can magnify the influence of this time by striving to be the best person you can be. This kua indicates that success is forthcoming, that friends will come to your aid, and that having somewhere to go or something to do will enhance your position. Even superior persons, no matter how careful they are, sometimes stray from the path of light, which is the path of abundant life. It is crucial that you realize when you have strayed from that path and that you turn back before going too far because otherwise you will "fall into the pit," meaning that you will suffer misfortune.

Having received this kua, reflect on your character and your actions, as well as the results that you have achieved, to see if you have strayed from the right path that will bring you the best and greatest benefits. If your life is not unfolding as you wish, it can only be because you have strayed from the path of light and need to make basic inner changes. If you do, you will find your way back to the right path, where you will again find great good fortune.

Because the light force is just returning, be gentle with yourself and avoid trying to accomplish too much too soon. To begin a small undertaking will meet with success. The return of the light force is a powerful time indeed, for all the beneficial forces of the Universe will now be exerting their influences in your behalf.

THE LINES

BOTTOM LINE: You have digressed slightly from the correct and honorable path, the path of abundant life, but, if you turn back quickly, you need not feel the slightest regret for this small misstep. If you ever find yourself thinking of acting in a manner that is in conflict with a path of high ethical and moral values, change those thoughts to beneficial ones and return to the correct path immediately. That will bring you great good fortune and will keep the dark force from exerting any sinister influence on your life. The dark force cannot have any effect on your life unless you invite it in with your thoughts and intentions. Be on your guard to avoid straying from the correct path in the future. If you turn back now, you will experience great good fortune.

LINE 2: You have strayed from the correct and honorable path and will experience negative consequences unless you turn back immediately. Deciding to do so is an act full of self-mastery. You will find it easier to realign yourself with the light force if you keep company with honorable individuals and avoid those who are unprincipled or dishonorable. If you turn back, you may also find that you must give up a relationship with a highly placed person or friend, but to do so will bring you good fortune.

LINE 3: This line indicates that you are a person who wavers back and forth between following the path of the superior person and that of the inferior person. There is danger in that weak behavior, because one day you may go too far on the path of darkness and find yourself unable to turn back. However, you will not suffer serious negative consequences at this time provided you turn back to the path of light without delay.

LINE 4: You are associating with inferior people who are leading you astray. Fortunately, you have a friend or associate of such great goodness and high principles that he or she can inspire you to turn back to the path of light, and turning back is the correct course for you. Of necessity, you will have to break with your dishonorable friends or associates, but that will be a small price to pay to ensure your future well-being. Although this line points to neither good fortune nor misfortune, aligning yourself with superior people is its own reward, as is turning away from unprincipled people.

LINE 5: You are in a commanding position but have strayed from the path of the superior person. Reflect on your inner state and your external situation to determine how and why this digression has occurred. When you identify it, gather all your inner reserves to turn back to the path of light and abundant life. You will never be sorry for having strayed from the path or for returning to it. However, if you fail to turn back, you will sincerely regret it.

TOP LINE: You have strayed too far from the path and have missed every opportunity to turn back. You will suffer inward misfortune because you have lost your self-respect and external misfortune because of the Universal law of cause and effect. The misfortune you will experience is for your benefit so that you will learn and grow from your mistakes. If you have started a forward push of any kind, you and your associates will meet with a defeat so devastating that a long time will pass before you recover.

25
WU WANG

Innocent Action,
Unexpected Misfortune

THE KUA

When we are born, we lack any conscious intention of doing either good or evil. It is only when our deliberate thought process begins that intent develops and innocence can be lost. Intent, by itself, is not harmful. It is only when our intentions are to deliberately hurt another or to act in a manner that is off the path of what is right, just, or good, that misfortune comes to us. In that case, you may as well not attempt anything because it will end either in failure or in a success that you will not enjoy or from which you will ultimately not benefit. If you would seek to influence others, follow the true inclination of your heart. Any deliberate action you take to influence others that does not arise from a sincere desire to benefit them lacks innocence and is therefore manipulative.

If we gain loyalty or allegiance through such manipulation, we must continue it afterward, or we will lose the loyalty or allegiance we gained. Such courses of action are emotionally exhausting and always end badly. To attract people naturally and effortlessly, we need only follow the true promptings of our hearts because the Universe has endowed us with a nature that is innately pure and good. The Universe does not provide good fortune or great rewards for those who do not act in accord with what is highest and best within them. If your intentions remain pure and you act without any ulterior thoughts of reward or advantages, you will be living in accord with your original nature. As a result, everything will work to your advantage and will bring supreme success and great good fortune to you. Of such stuff are true leaders made. This kua also depicts the condition of unexpected misfortune. Should that befall you, take heart, for it will ultimately pass away and work to your benefit. Superior persons take every turn of events, no matter how dire, and turn it into good fortune. So sure are they of their ability to do so that they will stake their very life upon it.

THE LINES

BOTTOM LINE: Here at the beginning, while your sincerity is still pure, your innocent actions will bring good fortune.

LINE 2: You are in a strong position. Carry out your responsibilities by completing each task for its own sake without consideration of reward. That will assure your success. Do good for the sake of doing good. Act in someone's best interest without expecting any praise or gain. If you act in accord with your own pure, unsullied, original nature, you will find advantage in everything you do, and good fortune will cling to you as your shadow clings to you in bright sunshine.

LINE 3: You have experienced or will experience misfortune or loss. The misfortune comes unexpectedly. Remain aware that you are a golden child of an eternal Universe in which everything that happens benefits you. To be a student of the Universe, which should be your goal, and to learn its ways, you must know that all the events that come into your life are lessons provided for you by a loving Universe, so that you may learn and grow.

You must confront the conditions and situations if you are to become strong and enduring. Such events are opportunities for growth and understanding. If you fail to look at them in that light, you will deprive yourself of the opportunity to learn from them and to obtain the great triumphs that are possible. Remember that the Universe, of which you are an inseparable part, wants you to be successful, wants you to be happy, and wants you to have all good things. Therefore, whatever befalls you is for the achievement of those goals.

LINE 4: You cannot lose something that is truly yours. If you are lamenting the loss of a friendship or relationship, do not worry, because if the person is truly meant for you, he or she will return. All that is necessary is that you be your pure, beautiful self; do not pay attention to what others say; and all else will be accomplished as a result of natural law.

LINE 5: A difficulty arises that does not seem to have been caused by anything you have said or done. You need not take action because it will pass in the natural course of time. Do not take any extreme measures to correct it because those measures will only work against you. This difficulty is a result of time rather than of your own doing, and, in time, it will pass away. If the difficulty is an illness, do not use any unusual or untried medicines or methods of treatment.

TOP LINE: The time for action is past. Even innocent action will not be successful. You must bide your time and wait for conditions to change. Fill your mind with happy thoughts, for this time will eventually change to another time when you will be able to make progress. When you believe the time has come, inquire of the oracle again to see if it is the right time to advance.

26
TA C'HU

Great Restraint

THE KUA

You want to make a forceful and aggressive advance, but someone or something is powerfully holding you back, or you should exert strong restraint on yourself at this time. You will not be serving your best interests if you try to advance now. Instead, wait until the restraining force has dissipated or the need for holding back has ended before making an advance. Do not waste this time of waiting in mere empty hoping, but fill it with useful activities carried out in the certainty that you will reach your goal. Then, when the period of restraint is over, you will be ready to advance. This time of restraint is beneficial in that it gives you an opportunity to cultivate your strengths and good qualities. While you wait, you will benefit from studying the great sayings of antiquity to be found in such books as the two volumes of *I Ching*

Wisdom (Power Press). The words of the great sages have survived for thousands of years because of their great value to the people and for the great wisdom they provide. You can use that wisdom to develop your own character and to gain valuable insights, and this will lead you to great success and good fortune. Only through such daily self-renewal will you be able to continue at the height of your powers. You will benefit from continuing to live according to the highest standards of conduct. The ancient text states that finding some way to enter public service at this time will work to your advantage. You will also benefit if you assist others to earn a living, and, when the period of holding back is past, if you turn your attention to finishing a project that you have started or by beginning a new project.

THE LINES

BOTTOM LINE: You are strong and correctly positioned, and you wish to make an advance, either alone or with your comrades. However, you face a threat from a highly placed person who will try to stop you. If you try to force your advance, misfortune will result. It will be to your advantage to impose restraint on yourself rather than being stopped by another. While you are in this period of holding back and waiting for a better time to move forward, you will benefit from making good use of your time by cultivating yourself and your good qualities as described in the opening paragraphs of this kua. Then, when the time of waiting is past, you may move forward.

LINE 2: You are strong and in a position of influence, and would like to make an advance. If you do, however, someone in authority will hold you back. Instead, restrain yourself and wait for a more favorable time, which will come. Any attempt you make to move forward now will meet with misfortune because the forces opposing you are too strong to overcome. During this time of great restraint, make good use of your time by cultivating yourself and your good qualities as described in the opening paragraphs of this kua. Then, when the time of holding back is past, you will be ready to move forward.

LINE 3: You have the necessary strength and are in a good position to move forward with your associate, who is a highly respected person who shares your aims. There is no reason why you should not move forward now, but be on the alert because there is danger at hand that calls for extreme caution. Spend every day practicing the skills needed for your advance while you also protect yourself from that danger. At this time, you will benefit from taking a trip or beginning a different project.

LINE 4: You hold a trusted position near the leader, but you must fulfill that trust by stopping a threat from a person in a subordinate position. The ancient text states that this threat may come from a person who is new to the group or just gaining power. Because of your own strength and position, you will be able to carry out this duty with no difficulty. However, you will have to take immediate measures to keep that person from growing stronger and becoming a more serious threat. Early action will bring you good fortune as well as a joyous feeling of accomplishment.

LINE 5: You are in a position of leadership but face danger from a subordinate or a person in a position of influence. You can put an end to that threat and block that adversary by taking immediate steps to change the adversary's intentions, restrict his or her power, or change his or her position. Taking such immediate and appropriate action will bring you good fortune.

TOP LINE: The time of restraint is past. You are deserving of the great power you hold. You may now move ahead toward the achievement of your goal; success and good fortune will be yours.

27
I

Providing Sustenance

THE KUA

This kua offers advice about providing food, financial resources, housing, education, spiritual guidance or information, material matters, and other forms of sustenance to
yourself and to others. When you take care of others, do not
weaken them with your generosity, for nothing is as powerful as necessity when it comes to strengthening the will and
creating a strong work ethic. Avoid depriving others of the benefits of providing for themselves, for unearned wealth always
works to destroy us. If you offer opportunities and education
to deserving people so they can earn their own livelihood, great
benefit will accrue to you and to them. What is more, they in
turn will later nourish others and thus society as a whole. Superior people are moderate and temperate in their eating,
drinking, and speech. Regarding food, take care to eat a healthy

diet, and to eat in moderation. In matters of income, finances, wealth, and other forms of material sustenance, do not permit others to provide for you if you can provide for yourself, for accepting such favors will only weaken and shame you.

This is not to say that you should not give or accept gifts, but that you should learn to become strong and independent and teach others to do the same. Wise individuals do not overreach themselves, overspend, or strive needlessly. If you observe the guidance of this kua, you will live long and well, prosper greatly, and be of major benefit to yourself and to others. Great good fortune and success will be yours.

THE LINES

BOTTOM LINE: The Chinese text for this line reads, "You let your magic tortoise go, and you look at me with the corners of your mouth drooping."

That refers to a legendary magic tortoise that was said to exist on dew and air alone, and was therefore completely independent. In effect, the statement means that you were able to provide for your own needs in the past but have given up your independence. Now, you are in the unfortunate position of looking to another for sustenance, which has brought loss of self-respect and unhappiness. Continuing in that manner will bring misfortune. There is also a possibility that you have either lost an opportunity or lost a friend. Make what amends you can and move on, having learned from your errors. This line advises you to make every effort to regain your independence, for that is the most important element missing in your life at this time.

LINE 2: The correct path followed by all right-thinking people is to provide and care for themselves and, in so doing, to become strong and independent. However, you have turned aside from that path and are seeking to have others provide for you. This is unworthy of you, and if you continue to look to others in that way, your situation will continue to worsen and you will incur ever-greater misfortune.

LINE 3: You are seeking to gratify yourself by indulging in forms of sustenance that do not nourish you and are unworthy of a superior person. That will bring misfortune. You are reeling from one pleasure to the next, seeking in vain what can never be obtained in that manner, for the frenzied pursuit of pleasures that gratify the senses never lead to the desired goal, which is happiness. Cease that behavior immediately.

LINE 4: Your intentions to benefit the people are honorable, for which you will be honored. Making an attempt to benefit the people is a big undertaking, so it would be wise for you to look for able people who can help you. In this case, the sincerity of your motives will bring you good fortune.

LINE 5: You are in a position of authority that carries with it a responsibility to help others, but you lack the strength and resources to do so. At this time, it is appropriate for you to seek help from a wealthy or highly placed person. If you persevere in seeking such help, you will experience good fortune, but do not attempt to reach any major goals at this time. Also, remain modest and do not take credit. That is the road to success.

TOP LINE: You bear the sole responsibility for providing sustenance for others, which is dangerous, because of the heavy responsibilities that comes with providing for other people. However, if you keep those obligations in mind at all times, as well as the potential danger, you will experience good fortune. You will benefit greatly if you undertake a lofty goal at this time.

28
TA KUO

Excess

THE KUA

This kua indicates that you have overused your power or have overindulged in excesses, which has created dangerous imbalances in your situation. These must be corrected immediately if a complete collapse is to be avoided. Everything in its proper measure benefits you, but the same thing, carried to excess, destroys you. The ancient text uses the example of the ridgepole that supports the roof of a house. A ridgepole that is thick and heavy at its center but weak at its ends will give way, and the entire structure will collapse unless immediate measures are taken. Similarly, if you can do anything to curb your overuse of power or reduce the excesses in this situation, do so immediately. However, even though the situation requires extraordinary measures, act gently and avoid using any forceful or aggressive measures, for too much force has already been at issue here. Great power is always best expressed in gentleness. Gaining insight into how to correct the imbalances will require thoughtful, penetrating reflection. Once you attain an inner mastery and understanding of the situation, any gentle action you take to correct it will succeed. If you can obtain help in correcting the excesses, do so. If not, carry on alone and do not lose heart. Maintain your good spirits and peace of mind, for this is a kua of success.

THE LINES

BOTTOM LINE: Extraordinary undertakings will succeed only if exceptional care is taken at the beginning. Everything in its beginning stages is always delicate, and a wrong move in any direction can bring disaster. It is better to be overly careful than not careful enough. Because you are just beginning, you must be flexible, cooperative, and persevering, as well as extremely cautious of every move you make. Avoid any overuse use of power and any excesses. If you act in accord with the guidance of this line, you will achieve success.

LINE 2: Renewal—a return of strength and power—is taking place. Take care not to overuse the new power that has come to you or soon will come to you. Without the required rest, the renewal will lack sufficient energy to sustain itself and will fail. During all periods of renewal, you must treat everything tenderly and with great care if the return is to produce a flowering. Avoid indulging in excesses of any kind. If you remain careful and moderate, everything you do will bring you success.

LINE 3: Indulging in excesses or the overuse of power has gone too far. As a result, you will experience misfortune. The situation cannot survive such abuses, and you are now threatened with imminent collapse. Neither friends nor associates will offer support. Take whatever steps you can to reduce the excesses and the overuse of power, but even with that prompt reduction, you cannot completely escape the dangerous consequences of the action already taken.

LINE 4: Indulging in excesses or the overuse of power has created a great imbalance in your situation, which is now extremely dangerous. However, help comes from an outside source, even a spiritual source. The ridgepole that was sagging to the breaking point is suddenly braced at its center, and good fortune results. Greet this unexpected and wonderful gift with reverence and gratitude, for without it, great misfortune would have befallen you. If help has come to you from subordinates, do not use your unexpected salvation for your own gain or honor, but bring benefit to everyone. You will shame yourself if you fail to honor those who assisted you in your time of need. Above all, be sure to express the greatest reverence for this timely intervention by All-That-Is.

LINE 5: A person thought to have exhausted his or her usefulness due to overindulgence or the overuse of power is experiencing an unexpected rebirth of energy and vitality, or a situation considered unproductive may be taking on new life. Although the recovery is wonderful, it will be short-lived because earlier excesses have taken too great a toll. Neither blame nor praise is attached to this line.

TOP LINE: The situation requires that you go forward, but, because you lack the strength and resources you need, failure will result. Nevertheless, no one will hold you responsible because it was necessary for you to proceed. Take heart. You are a golden child of a magical and alive Universe in which everything that happens benefits you. Remember that every ending contains a new beginning.

29
K'AN

Danger, The Abyss

THE KUA

The danger depicted in this kua is objective, meaning that it stems from an outside source. In most situations, you will be able to avoid the danger if you take appropriate action. However, if it cannot be overcome, you must simply endure it.

Danger does not always bring disaster nor does it always result in misfortune. The threat of danger has its important use because it sharpens your mind and prepares you to meet and cope with adversity. Danger makes you aware of weaknesses in your life, whether these have to do with our financial or business situation, our philosophical views, our domestic life, our relationships, or our social structure. With proper awareness, we can often avoid danger or even turn it to good use.

If you are aware of and understand the danger in this situation, you should inform others so that they too can prepare themselves, for you have a duty to alert them rather than keeping the information to yourself. The ancient text urges you to teach others not just about the danger that now threatens, but also to share with them any spiritual wisdom that you may possess.

This kua is known as "The Abyss," which refers to a pit. To escape it—to avoid falling into the pit—you must first take every precaution not to be overcome by it, and then act immediately to extricate yourself or eliminate it. If you remain true to your highest and best principles and use your intuition to penetrate to the source of this threat, you will gain inner mastery over it. Once you have done so, any action you take will naturally succeed.

THE LINES

BOTTOM LINE: You have turned away from what you know to be the path of an honorable life and have engaged in dangerous behaviors. Because you have escaped the danger so far, you have convinced yourself that you are safe, but such is not the case. The danger has now overtaken you, and you have fallen or soon will fall into what the ancient text describes as "The Pit." This will have serious negative consequences. Because you are weak and lacking in resources and support and because the danger is so strong, you will find it difficult to overcome the danger. Your only course of action at this time is to use whatever resources you have to perceive the source of the danger and to act immediately to correct it. Nonetheless, the pronouncement of this line is misfortune. Take heart. You are a part of the Universe, and as such, protected.

LINE 2: You are strong and your position carries some authority, but the danger is too great to overcome, and you will be able to achieve only a small success at this time. You will meet with disaster if you try to attain any major goals now. The wisdom of this line is that you should not seek to accomplish what is impossible, but instead focus your attention fully on surviving and extricating yourself from the danger.

LINE 3: Danger surrounds you, and moving in any direction will only increase the threat. You may find it difficult to sit and wait, but the only correct action at this time is to take no action. The opportunity is soon coming that will allow you to escape the danger. Watch for it, and when you perceive it, act on it immediately.

LINE 4: You are close to a strong person in authority and can be of help to that person in this time of danger. Be sure to offer practical help such as time or resources, and give it freely, without any expectation of personal gain. If you make a show of it and boast about how important your help is, it will only work against you. Instead, offer your assistance as modestly and unobtrusively as possible. You will receive great credit for your help.

LINE 5: The danger is not strong enough to overwhelm you, but it is still serious. Although you are strong and occupy a position of leadership, avoid taking any forceful or aggressive action. If you follow the path of no resistance at this time, you will perceive a way out, and the danger will then fade away. Perhaps it is your excessive ambition that has brought about this danger. After it passes, adopt less forceful strategies for attaining your goals. What is attained by force must be maintained by force, which is exhausting and usually results in the loss of what has been attained.

TOP LINE: You are trapped in danger and will see no end to your problems until much time has passed. Perhaps this danger, which is too serious for you to overcome at this time, was brought about by your decision to stray from the path of honor and integrity. You can hasten your deliverance from the danger if you return to the path of abundant life, which is the path of honor and integrity. To do so, you must lead a life of high ethical and moral values and act with only the highest and best motives. The pronouncement of this line is misfortune.

30
LI

Clarity,
Brightness, Adherence

THE KUA

All things in the Universe cling to that which gives them life and cause them to thrive. Thus do flames cling to wood, plants to earth, and newborns to their mother's breast. And so too must we humans, being spiritual beings, cling to the spiritual essence of the Universe if we are to thrive. This is the kua of brightness, and to maintain the brightness of your essence, your intelligence, reason, clarity, and spirituality, you must refresh yourself every day from the Universal fount of spiritual wisdom. If you do not, your light will grow dim, and you will stray from the path of abundant life, which means that you will continue to live, but not abundantly. Li also represents fire, the sun, and nature in all its great radiance. Like fire, its motion is directed upward. Because this kua is the trigram of Li doubled, it signifies exceptional intelligence, reason, clarity, and spiritual wisdom that will guide you in following the path of what is right, good, and just.

To live in the fullness of life, you must follow the rhythms of life, giving and taking, inhaling and exhaling, sleeping and waking, and absorbing spiritual wisdom and giving it out. Be like the apple tree that absorbs nourishment from the earth and freely gives its fruit to all who pass by. If you are to share your light and wisdom, you must first cultivate light and wisdom. Refresh yourself in the springs of wisdom from the oldest teachings that have survived for thousands of years, for, as the ancient text states, "The great man, by perpetuating his brightness, illumines the four quarters of the world."

To complete and perfect your cycle of learning and teaching, share the wisdom you gain. By following the path of the superior person, which is the path of abundant life, you will enjoy good friends, good health, prosperity, peace, harmony, and possessions in great measure, as well as supreme success and great good fortune. But know also that the same Universal law that brings you these gifts will remove them from you if you stray from the path of an honorable life. The pronouncement for you of this kua is good fortune and success.

THE LINES

BOTTOM LINE: You are strong and just starting out. You want to press forward quickly but are confused and uncertain about the correct path to follow. If you live in a state of perpetual hurry, you will never attain composure, and stress will exhaust you. Composure is a state in which the mind is settled, calm, and tranquil. If you can attain that state, you will be able to act without stress, and will, therefore, make no mistakes. Take your time. Be patient. Do not let yourself be steered off your course by outside influences, but remain steadfast in your determination to reach your goal. During this time of new beginnings, the first actions you take will determine the success or failure of what is to come later. Remember that character is the bowstring from which we shoot the arrows of the future. We must renew our efforts each day to shape our character, for nothing else is as important to our life and success. Proceed with great reverence in your heart for All-That-Is and remain steadfast in your intent to reach your goal in the right way.

LINE 2: The keynote of this line is moderation without extremes. Following the middle path will lead you to success. Do not act hastily, but calmly and with deliberation. Use your intelligence to make a detailed plan for achieving your goal. You are now planting the seeds that will determine your success. As is true for the beginnings of all things, great care must be taken if planting is to lead to harvesting. Be sure that you are remaining true to what is highest and best within you, do not use any extreme measures, and you will naturally achieve supreme good fortune.

LINE 3: This line is an indication that an ending is near—perhaps life, as in old age or severe illness, or a project that is coming to an end, a relationship that is fading, or anything that is diminishing or dying out like the ending of each day, which sees the light fade as the Earth turns and the Sun disappears. In this time of great brilliance and clarity, you should be rejoicing and giving thanks for all that you have. Instead, you are lamenting and complaining like an old person who fears the approach of death. Such behavior shows that you have lost your clarity and, unless you mend your behavior, will bring misfortune in its wake as surely as water flows downhill.

To persons of true understanding, it makes no difference whether death comes early or late. Their sense of the transitory nature of life does not drive them to seek out amusements so they can feel they are enjoying life while it lasts, nor does their understanding that life inevitably diminishes cast them into melancholy or sadness, and thereby spoil the time remaining to them. Such people feel no fear of death, which is only an instant of transition, like walking through a doorway from one room to the next, and is no more remarkable than any other moment in time.

Take hold of yourself, and remember that you are an indestructible child of a golden Universe in which everything that happens benefits you. Every ending contains a new beginning. Be strong, be cheerful, be brave, be steadfast, be full of faith that all is well, and you will turn this time of ending into good fortune. Remember, it is Universal law that whatever is now fading will find a renewal in another beginning. Be happy.

LINE 4: You are a strong person but given to rash behavior. At this time, your rashness either has created or will create a brief success that will flare up, die out, and be forgotten, or else you will flare into popularity, only to fade quickly and disappear into obscurity. To produce long-lasting effects, you must cultivate an unshakable ability to endure inwardly as well as outwardly in the undertakings that you pursue.

Enduring means continuing to the end in the face of obstacles, pain, fatigue, frustration, opposition, or hardship, and even enduring in the good times. Do whatever you can to avoid rash, thoughtless, or extreme action. The plan you are now contemplating will be short-lived, so either abandon it or develop another one that has a better chance of coming to fruition and producing lasting results.

LINE 5: This is a time of great clarity when you can reflect on your past carefully to see what results your actions have produced. There is a strong indication that this look backward will cause you to feel remorse and heartache for the errors you have made and the suffering you have caused others.

Although this self-examination may make you feel great sadness, it will also bring about a real change of heart. If you carry out the good intentions that arise out of this time of recollection, good fortune will come to you.

TOP LINE: Others are obstructing or trying to interfere with your striving for clarity and your determination to follow the path of honor. You are in a commanding position to go out and subdue the opposition, and doing so will bring you good fortune. Dismiss or distance yourself from those who are leading this effort to obstruct you, or punish them so that they commit no further offenses. Regarding their followers, deal with them leniently, but still forcefully enough to deter future transgressions. In this time of great clarity, it is essential that you adhere to the highest standards of honor and right action.

3 1
HSIEN

Attraction, Influence

THE KUA

The universal force of attraction draws people together for every purpose. Such coming together is a joyous event and brings great success. Creating and consolidating long-lasting relationships will bring good fortune at this time. If you continue to conduct yourself in ways that are receptive, inviting, modest, and devoid of ulterior motives, you will see your influence grow, and people will be encouraged to approach you. However, if your motives are selfish, dishonest, or fail to stem from an intention to benefit all concerned, misfortune will result, and your relationships will prove so unrewarding that it would be better if you had not met at all.

In this time of attraction and influence, you will find it easy to enlist the aid of helpers, or to attract those to whom you are attracted. You need only be openly receptive and

encouraging to them. Once you have created those relationships, binding them will bring good fortune. If you are
a man who is seeking to attract a woman, avoid acting forcefully or trying to dominate her. Instead, be low-key and yielding in your attitude and behavior. If you are a woman, be
open, receptive, and inviting.

THE LINES

BOTTOM LINE: The attraction is in its first stage. Be
open, receptive, and modest. Avoid any aggressive behavior.
Act out of your higher nature rather than your lower. Any
attitude of self-importance or arrogance will repel rather
than attract. Because this is the time of attraction, if you are
relaxed, calm, and at ease with yourself, the relationship will
develop naturally, as an outcome of Universal law. You will
find it helpful to bring a gift or offering. The gift itself is of
little importance; rather, it is your sincerity in giving it that
will matter.

LINE 2: The attraction is growing and becoming more
intense and exciting, but taking any action at this time will
lead to misfortune. If you remain open to the possibilities but
avoid taking any action that would signify commitment, you
will have good fortune. Wait until you have a much clearer indication that the relationship will be beneficial and worth-

while before committing yourself. During this time of waiting, focus on improving your character.

LINE 3: You are now feeling or soon will feel a strong attraction to join with someone who is in a stronger position than you are. It may be that this person will be of great value to you in business matters or will possibly present a new love relationship. There is also a possibility that this person will ask you to do something that is not appropriate for a person of high ethical and moral values. Even though your desire to create a relationship with that person may be so strong that you may be tempted to grant his or her request, to do so will be an error that will lead to misfortune for you. If you depart from the path of the superior person, you will lose respect for yourself, and the person with whom you want to join will see you as a person of low character. For remaining true to what is highest and best within you, you will earn your own self-respect as well as the respect of the person with whom you want to join.

LINE 4: You are close to those in authority and in a position to be a strong, positive influence. If you deliberately try to manipulate your associates or the person or persons you wish to attract, your efforts will come to nothing and your influence will decrease. Instead, use this time to cultivate and improve your character. Your natural abilities and strengths will bring about the influence and attraction you seek effortlessly and naturally. Also, everyone who enters your sphere of influence, not just those upon whom you focus your full attention, will come under the spell of your good character and kindhearted intentions.

LINE 5: You are in a position of leadership and influence, and you have a strong desire for greater influence. Because you are well intentioned and inwardly strong, the results you produce are beneficial. If you remain true to your inner beliefs in this time of attraction, you will naturally produce results consistent with your intentions to benefit those who are aligned with you. True goodness means that your intentions are always well intended and never meant to cause harm. To maintain those intentions, each day you must resolve anew to follow the path of the superior person by striving constantly to improve your character. If you persevere in your efforts, you will find within you a wellspring of joy that will refresh and renew you every day of your life, and good fortune and success will be yours. The responsibilities of your position are causing you to act rigidly and strictly but still justly. Although you will meet with some resistance, the overall effect will be advantageous.

TOP LINE: You are attempting to influence people through words alone. When spoken by the right person at the right time, words can be powerfully effective. However, the indication here is that you lack the power or influence needed to use words alone. Through words and deeds, you move Heaven and Earth, and, by your words and deeds, you create good fortune and misfortune. That is why you should always be careful of everything you say and do. Furthermore, all words and deeds spring from within, so, if your heart is pure and your motivation is rooted in your inner integrity, your words will be direct and powerful, and your actions will produce far-reaching, beneficial effects. If your heart is not as it should be, you will not escape falling into an abyss of misfortune that you will have created. During this time of attraction, your success in attracting those you are seeking out will require more than just words. If you have anything at your disposal that you can offer as an incentive, do so, and you will be successful.

32
HÊNG

Endurance, Long-Lasting

THE KUA

There are two meanings to this kua. The first meaning is long duration or long-lasting. Duration is a state that is not worn down by anything. Whether your question to the oracle concerns personal or business relationships, ownership, conditions, or situations, the answer is that the topic under consideration will have long duration. The second meaning of the kua is perseverance. Because the topic under consideration will have a long life, you must develop a deep reservoir of perseverance that will see you through to the attainment of your goal and will provide you with support in the face of pain, fatigue, frustration, opposition, or hardship, and even during the best of times. Perseverance means to continue to the end. Once you have established the inner condition of perseverance, you will be able to reach your goal, overcome any obstacle, and bear up in any situation. Your perseverance will lead you to success.

Superior persons stand firm in the face of changing times and do not permit anything or anyone to deter them from achieving their goals.

That does not mean that you should ignore changing conditions or never revise your plans in keeping with such changing conditions. Rather, it means that you should not follow each new, passing fad. Success will come to you if you begin anew at every ending, cultivate long-lasting strengths of character, and develop inner consistency. When you behave according to those principles, others will not find fault with you. Above all, remain true to your inner resolve to follow the path of the superior person. That inner resolve will be the core of your success, for it will be the ground out of which all your actions spring. The guidance of this kua is that the topic of your question will have a long life, and by being persevering, you will achieve your success.

THE LINES

BOTTOM LINE: You are hurrying to try to accomplish something that can only be accomplished slowly and with attention to detail. Your hurried state will cause you to fail in important areas. The correct way to make something strong and enduring is to nurture it gradually and over a long period of time. If you think of an oak tree, it is big and strong, but it only achieved its immensity over a considerable period of time. You should think of achieving your goal in that manner. It is commendable to push yourself to new heights because this can increase your powers so you can reach ever-greater success. However, if you strive to reach unrealistic or unattainable goals at this time, you will court disaster and failure. Instead, satisfy yourself with achieving smaller goals for now. Superior people do not overreach themselves, overspend, or strive needlessly, and thus they enjoy a lifetime of success. The current situation finds you in a weak position, and therefore, your attempt to forge ahead quickly is rash and will come to nothing. Instead, hold back at this time, and turn your attention to devising a new but more cautious, low-key, and well-thought-out approach that you can carry out with perseverance over time.

LINE 2: You are strong and in a central position, and you have the support of the person or persons in authority. Now is a good time for you to undertake a small project, but do not use great strength or power because this will drain your energy and is inappropriate for this period of time that requires endurance and perseverance. You may lack the resources you need to accomplish your goal, so take careful inventory of what you have at your disposal and carry out your planning with equal care. If you avoid extreme measures and follow a moderate, middle-of-the-road approach, you will have success.

LINE 3: There is an indication that you are lacking in certain important qualities of character. This lack causes you to remain at the mercy of hope and fear. It is as if you are a cork bobbing up and down on the ocean with no real control over what happens to you. As a result, you are continually humiliated. If you fail to make the effort to improve your character, you will continue to suffer disgrace. Given that this is the time of duration, it is essential that you see your project through to the end and persevere in being a person of the utmost integrity.

LINE 4: What you seek is not available at this time or in this place. It is useless for you to persist in trying to reach your goal at this time.

LINE 5: You are in a position of leadership and have the support of your followers. This is a time for you to be strong, to persevere in acting according to the highest principles, and to bear up in the face of adversity. If you do all these things, you will set a good example for your followers, and good fortune will come to you. However, if you fail to assert yourself at this time when strength is required, you will invite misfortune.

TOP LINE: You are acting hastily and impatiently. If you live in a state of perpetual hurry, you can never attain the calm, tranquil, settled state of mind that brings success. Those who can attain that state are able to act without stress, so they make no mistakes. Constant hurrying destroys all sense of calm and leads to exhaustion, illness, and even premature death. If you slow down, nurture yourself by following the path of the superior person, and cultivate patience and endurance, natural law will bring about the achievement of your goal. If you continue in a restless, hasty manner, misfortune will result.

33
TUN

Withdrawal, Retreat

THE KUA

The forces of darkness are growing stronger. To protect yourself, remove yourself, your assets, and everything important to you from the situation. Because this is a condition of the time, it will pass away of its own accord, but while it continues, withdrawal is the only appropriate course. It is through retreat that you will achieve your success. However, do not let your withdrawal be rash, abrupt, hasty, or frantic and disorganized.

Instead, act with caution after you have devised a carefully thought-out plan to remove yourself and your assets from the situation. If you are involved in a conflict, your retreat is not a surrender, but rather a strategic withdrawal that will allow you to replenish your forces, conserve what you have, and develop a new plan that will lead to victory. Avoid exhausting yourself or depleting your assets at this time. Nor should you make any all-out efforts to force your advance, for they will fail. If a person or group wants you to join them, it will be in your best interests to gently extricate yourself from them and the situation, and then to make yourself unavailable to them. Following the guidance of this kua will lead to your success.

THE LINES

BOTTOM LINE: You lack the strength and resources to accomplish your goal, and danger threatens. Do all you can to remove yourself and your assets from the situation, or, if you cannot, at least take no action whatsoever until the danger passes. Do not attempt an advance, for that will only jeopardize you and your assets. You have a highly placed friend on whom you can rely for advice or assistance.

LINE 2: You are in a good position but lack the power to accomplish your goal. You also have highly placed friends on whom you can and should rely for advice and help. Take immediate action to remove yourself and your assets from the situation as best you can. Be inwardly persevering in your intention to reach your goal, but do not attempt to move ahead at this time.

If a subordinate is making forceful efforts to become associated with you, assess the situation carefully to see if you would benefit from permitting that connection. It would be appropriate to do another reading for guidance in making that decision.

LINE 3: You have an opportunity to withdraw yourself and your assets from the situation, but that would leave your subordinates in jeopardy. You have a duty to protect them, and to do so will bring you good fortune, but nothing great can be accomplished at this time. If a person or group is persistent in exerting pressure on you to join in an alliance, you may benefit from doing so because continuing to resist may drain your energy or assets. However, nothing of great value will come of such an alliance.

LINE 4: Although your position is not strong at this time, you have the strength needed to withdraw yourself and your assets from the situation, and you should do so without delay. You must also withdraw your friendship and support. Do not withdraw with anger or with any intent to hurt the person or persons from whom you are withdrawing, but withdraw with courtesy and caution. Your subordinates will suffer because of your action, but you can do nothing to help them in this situation.

LINE 5: You have the strength, assets, resources, and position to withdraw yourself and your assets from the situation in a friendly manner. Do so at once. Do not let yourself be held back by others or by their arguments. Withdraw in an easygoing manner that will not arouse resentment. If you maintain that stance, you will have good fortune.

TOP LINE: You are in an ideal position to withdraw yourself and your assets from the situation completely, and to do so will bring you happiness and success. Carry out your retreat in a friendly manner, but firmly and without delay.

34
TA CHUANG

Great Power, Great Strength

THE KUA

The lower trigram's three solid lines indicate great power and strength, and the lines want to advance. Added to this already great power is the aggressive upward movement of the upper trigram, which symbolizes thunder. The two trigrams taken together represent an irresistible force. Because you know that progress is certain, you should have only one goal: to advance in an appropriate manner. Before you set forth, be sure to pause and make certain that your actions are in accord with what is just, right, and honorable. Then you will move forward with good intentions, and only along paths that are in keeping with good conduct and are socially acceptable. Avoid any action or behavior that would violate these standards. Conduct yourself at all times in a courteous, friendly and dignified manner. Most importantly, behave with honor and integrity. Such conduct will ensure that after you have made your advance and achieved your goal, you will be able to enjoy the results of your success rather than exposing yourself to criticism. Your success is certain, so be sure to pursue it only by acting in ways that will bring you honor and respect.

THE LINES

BOTTOM LINE: You possess great power and are poised to advance forcefully, but this is not the correct course of action. Pushing forward forcibly at this time will certainly bring misfortune. This is a moment for patient waiting, not force. Use this time to assess your situation and plan for the time when you will be able to make the advance you desire. It will come soon, but be sure that your goal is honorable, that your effort will not go against the standards of social acceptability, and that you have within you the endurance to carry through to the end. Despite the great power at your disposal, now is a time to wait. If you do, you will reap success and good fortune in the end.

LINE 2: You are strong, in a powerful position, and enjoy the support of those in power. You may move forward at this time, but be careful because there is danger here. You should carefully study the situation before making your move. After you have taken this careful look, you may move forward with caution. Bear in mind that if you compromise your principles or act out of unworthy motives, your forward progress will come to naught. On the other hand, continuing to act honorably and with good intentions will assure that your advance will meet with good fortune and success.

LINE 3: You are in a strong position to move forward, and you also have the support of those in authority, so your success in this effort is assured. In such a situation, an inferior person might use his or her strength to make an aggressive advance, but that would only create complications. Superior people, on the other hand, know that they should use their strength gently because then they can move forward without arousing resentment or resistance. If you adopt a course of action that is too aggressive, you will bring danger to yourself. You may be tempted to boast about your position of strength, but that would only work against you, for boasting is always a sure indication that a person feels inferior and is trying to inflate his or her stature. Instead, let the achievement of your goal speak for itself. This line counsels you to move gently toward your success while avoiding making any show of it.

LINE 4: You are strong and in an excellent position, and you have the help of those in authority if you need it. You may now move forward with full confidence, but be careful not to abuse your strength by using it to excess. The path ahead of you will be smooth, and you will easily overcome whatever small obstacles remain. If you make a show of your strength, you will create problems that do not now exist, so be sure to move ahead gently and with the intentions of benefiting everyone concerned. Treat those who help you honorably. If you follow this guidance, you will achieve success without any complications arising, and you will move ahead to ever-greater accomplishments.

LINE 5: You are in an excellent position and have the support of your associates if you need it, so you can accomplish your goal easily if you move forward now. You do not have to be aggressive or stubborn in your advance. If you move ahead too forcefully when a situation does not call for it, you will meet with resistance and resentment. If you move gently toward your goal, no one will hold anything against you, and you will enjoy your success to the fullest.

TOP LINE: You have moved ahead too forcefully and have therefore become overwhelmed by complications. Neither backward nor forward motion will extricate you. Instead, you must come to a standstill, compose and center yourself, examine the situation so you can uncover the source of the problem, and then solve it. If you do, you will free yourself from the complications and enjoy success and good fortune.

35
CHIN

Great Progress

THE KUA

This is a wonderful time when the light force is powerfully in the ascendancy. The coupling of expansion and great clarity in this kua, which is symbolized by the sun blazing down on the earth and spreading its life-giving rays, brings tremendous forward progress. Great achievements can now be accomplished, and great merit will be richly rewarded. If you are part of a group, be loyal and generous, share the credit for your accomplishments, overlook the faults of others, and forgive even intentional violations. By bringing a benefit to your friends or associates, you too will be well rewarded. In this time of great progress, do nothing to disturb the upward spiral of your success. Rather, be like the sun at midday: shine brightly, give generously, and enjoy your rapid, easy progress. As always, if you follow the path of the superior person and act only out of honor, thoughtfulness, and kindness, all that you seek will come to you easily, marvelously, and in complete fullness. In this time of great progress, you will be richly rewarded and will receive the respect and admiration of those in authority.

THE LINES

BOTTOM LINE: The time of rapid, easy progress is just beginning. You are not yet strong enough to take full advantage of it, so your best course now is to prepare for the time when you will be able to move rapidly and easily toward your goal. That time will come soon. While you wait, develop your character. Also, working diligently in your chosen field will strengthen your position. You have a friend who is not the leader but who is in a position of authority; confer with him or her.

LINE 2: You are well positioned but lack help from someone in authority with whom you are connected. That lack of support and your inability to make progress are causing you worry. Nonetheless, this is a time of great progress, so your position will allow you to make headway even though you lack the support you seek. If you refuse to lose heart but instead continue your efforts, you will ultimately receive much help from the person in question here. It is essential that you continue to act honorably, for that is the basis of your connection to him or her. Perhaps an older woman will assist you. Be on the lookout for her, for she can be of great help to you.

LINE 3: You are in a position to advance and can do so safely because you are in accord with the aims of those in authority. You also enjoy the support of your colleagues and associates. Any regret you feel about not being able to make progress on your own will disappear in the light of your accomplishments. During this time of rapid, easy advance, you can resolve misunderstandings that may have arisen and that may be blocking your progress. Good fortune lies ahead.

LINE 4: There is a danger here in that you may have strayed from the path of honor by engaging in devious and underhanded behavior. Such behavior is unworthy of you and your position and can only lead to failure. Because this is a time of brightness, any action you take that violates what is just, right, and principled will be found out, and you will be censured for it. You have a good relationship with the leader. Maintain that relationship, act forthrightly and fairly, avoid ulterior motives, and you will achieve success.

LINE 5: During this time of rapid, easy progress, do not be concerned with success or failure, gain or loss. Ultimately, everything we humans seek and cherish will come to nothing, just as even the finest clothes one day turn to rags. You are not your gain, nor are you your loss, for all gains and losses pass away at the moment of death. If you have suffered any losses, do not be concerned or disheartened. Instead, press on, for you will achieve great accomplishments. All causes for regret will disappear, and joy will come to you. If you act in that manner, you will obtain great influence, which, in this situation, will serve you far better than material gains.

TOP LINE: Advances can be carried too far, and, because you are now using force to try to increase your success, you may actually turn it into failure. Take great care as you proceed from this point on, for there is some danger in the situation. At this time, you may act forcefully to bring your associates into line, but avoid doing so with outsiders, for that will bring on the danger.

36
MING I

Persecution

THE KUA

A weak, petty adversary, that could be either a person or a group, is bent on harming, persecuting, or victimizing you. Many possible motives, such as resentment, jealousy, the adversary's belief that he or she is protecting another, or sheer malice, may exist. Perhaps your adversary may fear that you will undermine their status or resources, or establish a relationship with someone he or she may not want you to have a relationship with, or accomplish something that they see as potentially damaging or detrimental. Their persecution is an attempt to undermine you and weaken your position so you will not be able to accomplish what they fear. If you are to maintain your position and succeed in attaining your goal during this time of adversity, persevere in what you know to be right, and behave with the utmost discretion in every way. Most importantly, avoid calling attention to your wealth, resources, ability and intelligence, or you will risk antagonizing the adversary further. Continue to follow the path of honor and integrity, and act always from your higher nature rather than your lower. Be modest and unassuming. Avoid claiming credit for your accomplishments, but share your credit with others. Do not abandon your goal unless you believe that you might cause irreparable harm to yourself or to others if you persist. The best way to guarantee your success in this situation is to bide your time; to go about your affairs with the utmost discretion and caution; and to avoid any forceful, aggressive, or extreme behaviors or actions that could arouse resentment or resistance. Be content with any minor gains you can make while remaining inwardly perservering in reaching your goal.

THE LINES

BOTTOM LINE: You have been soaring too high and have attracted the adverse attention of others who will persecute or who are persecuting you. Adopting a low profile will protect you from attacks and injury. Going on a trip at this time will also be beneficial, for, according to the principle of "out of sight, out of mind," your absence will work to your benefit. Follow the guidance given in the opening paragraph, for it will stand you in good stead during this time of persecution. The ancient text speaks of fasting for three days to gain the clarity you need to see your way through a situation. Fasting is an excellent way to achieve clarity, but it must be done in the right way. Consult an expert and follow his or her advice about how to fast. Those around you will gossip about your fast, but that is to be expected when people do not understand fasting and its benefits.

LINE 2: Those who are persecuting you have succeeded so well that you will find it almost impossible to make any progress. Draw on your strengths and resources to help not only yourself but also others who may be under attack. Such a course of action will bring good fortune. Do not allow the circumstances to overwhelm you, but respond in as low-key a manner as possible while still remaining true to your principles. Slander will always fade and die out on its own if we refuse to try to defend or justify ourselves with angry retorts. We can spend our entire lives tracking down attacks and defending ourselves, but it is better to simply go on with our own affairs. The best defense against slander is to live the life of the superior person and to let our actions and conduct speak for us. This line has good fortune attached to it, so be of good cheer, for you will survive the attack, and all will be well.

LINE 3: You have overcome or will soon overcome those in power who have been trying to injure you. This victory appears to have come about by chance, but, of course, there is no "chance" about it at all, for "coincidence" and "chance" do not exist in our Universe.

The Universe, which governs and controls everything, has intervened directly on your behalf. Once the opposing forces have been defeated, if they have not been already, and you have gained control, do not rush to institute reforms, but take time to develop a careful plan for the changes you want to bring about. Do not take credit for or flaunt your victory, or you may turn it into a defeat.

LINE 4: You have made or will soon make a breakthrough in understanding why you are being persecuted. Remove yourself immediately from the situation safely and discreetly in order to protect yourself from the persecution which is now strong.

LINE 5: You are being persecuted by someone but are reluctant to give up trying to achieve your goal. If you are to achieve success, you must maintain absolute inner integrity while avoiding outward displays of any kind, including flaunting your abilities or intelligence, undertaking high-profile initiatives, or engaging in displays of wealth. The guidance in the opening paragraph of this kua will be of great value to you in achieving your goal. The ancient text tells of Prince Chi, who feigned insanity to keep from being killed by the tyrant emperor Chou Shin. This worked because Chou Shin did not feel threatened by Prince Chi and therefore saw no need to kill him. Prince Chi did fake insanity, but at the same time he remained true to his inner convictions but did not let them show. In essence, you must lay low for now.

TOP LINE: You have abused your power and used it to hurt others. Anyone who commits thoughtless and intentionally hurtful acts will reap shame and humiliation.

37
CHIA JÊN

The Family, The Group

THE KUA

This kua indicates an influence now or soon to come in your life that has to do with a family or group of which you are or will be a part. Being part of a family or group will enable you to accomplish much more than you can alone and will bring you good fortune. Keep in mind that you should conduct yourself as a person of honor and integrity at all times, not just with members of your family or group, but with everyone. Such behavior will bring honor to your family or group and will also earn you their honor and respect, which is a great credit to you, and one that you should work diligently to obtain. You can achieve that respect by living up to the model of the superior person in every way. Superior people live up to their word, meaning that they do what they say they will do and they always speak the truth. Also, their words and actions are always in harmony, and, if they say that being trustworthy is important, they should always be trustworthy. This kua depicts the inner structure and dynamics of a family or group. When all members fulfill their respective duties and show the appropriate love and respect to one another, the family or group functions efficiently and harmoniously. Families and groups should establish common traditions and beliefs, meaning that they should agree to continue to uphold honorable principles in common, rather than adopting every passing trend, and that they are loyal and dedicated to all the other members. Internal conflict or dissension weakens the power of families and groups to act as a unit in overcoming external dangers.

THE LINES

BOTTOM LINE: Because the family or group is in its formative stages, now is the time to establish firm rules so that all members will know their duties and what they can and cannot do. If you plan well at the outset, you will avoid mistakes and regrets later. As at the beginning of everything, careful planning is essential if goals are to be reached. Here you have the opportunity to create the rules, guidelines, and structures that will make it possible to bring about exactly what you are envisioning. You are the architect of your dream, and you can make changes with ease at this time because you are still at the beginning. Creating a strong image in your mind of what you want and communicating it to all who belong to your group or family so that they can engage in a concerted effort will be of immense benefit in reaching your goal. Developing clear, well-developed guidelines now will prevent regrets or remorse later.

LINE 2: You hold an important position in the family or group. Although you are not the leader, your present position is appropriate for you at this time. Your most important task now is to focus all your energies on your main duties, which are to nurture and maintain the family's or group's health and well-being. At all costs, avoid any use of force, for it will work against you. Do not give in to whims or impulses that will cause you to neglect your duty. If you fulfill your responsibilities conscientiously, good fortune will come to you.

LINE 3: You have dealt so severely with a person or persons in your family or group that your action may lead to danger. You will feel regret or remorse, but good fortune will come. In this situation, it was a better course to overreact than to be too permissive. There is an indication that some members are being lazy or irresponsible. If you permit such behavior to continue, negative consequences will result. Discipline is always essential if a family or group is to remain cohesive and engaged in the concerted effort needed to reach the goals that have been set.

LINE 4: You have shown yourself to be a great treasure for your family or group. You will bring great good fortune to everyone, including yourself. If you are a woman, you are responsible for your group's or family's well-being, and, because you are such a treasure, everyone will benefit. In financial matters, a balance between income and expenditures guarantees well-being and security because, as the saying goes, "Out of debt, out of danger." Do not spend more than you have, for living on credit equals enslavement. Because all periods of prosperity are inevitably followed by periods of decline, superior persons use prosperous times to prepare for declines. If you are in the habit of spending all that you have, any emergency will find you unprepared. Such poor planning is an invitation to disaster because it will destroy your well-being, as well as your family's or group's.

LINE 5: You are in a position of authority that brings with it serious responsibilities. Use your position and your influence to bring good fortune to all, thus demonstrating noble and wise leadership. Because people look up to you, your behaviors and actions influence everyone in your family or group at every moment. Take time to be generous and car-ing, and look for ways to benefit not just individuals but the group or family as a whole. Because you always act with good intentions, others will have no reason to fear you, and by being a good leader, you will achieve success and good fortune for yourself and for them.

TOP LINE: You have risen high, and you command the respect of all because of your sincerity, inner worth, and noble qualities of leadership and character. These worthy attributes bring good fortune to everyone. Take on full responsibility for your family or group's well-being, for you have the power and influence to benefit everyone in positive ways. If you lead by example, you will enjoy great good fortune.

38
K'UEI

Alienation,
Division

THE KUA

At this time, your friendship or relationship with a person or group has degenerated into unfriendliness, hostility, or alienation. This may be due to something you did or said, or perhaps someone else is instigating it. Most likely, the problem is the result of a misunderstanding. To correct the misunderstanding, be willing to take the blame, be tolerant of the other side's feelings, overlook mistakes, and forgive even deliberate violations.

Do not attempt a major resolution of the situation at this time, because you will meet with failure and only further alienation will result. Only minor gains can be made, or small issues resolved at this time, and you must content yourself with those.

Do not lose heart. Remain hopeful and cheerful. If the relationship is based on a real affinity, it will right itself in time, provided you treat it with careful attention and continue to follow the path of the superior person.

THE LINES

BOTTOM LINE: The division and alienation are just beginning. If you have lost a relationship with someone, there is no need to run after that person because if you are supposed to be with that person, he or she will return of his or her own accord. If you are not supposed to be with that person, the union will not take place, no matter what you do. Because of your honorable character, you can heal the growing separation between you and the other person. He or she also is honorable, so, despite the antagonism that has arisen, the high principles you share will see you through. You need not feel remorse or regret, because the relationship will right itself and will be stronger and better than ever after the time of alienation is past. Should you meet or have dealings with the people who have brought about the alienation, be on your guard, but do not avoid them, for some good will come from the encounter.

LINE 2: Because of the alienation that has occurred, it is almost impossible for you to meet openly with the person from whom you are alienated, even though you may both desire it. If either of you can arrange a meeting in an out-of-the-way place where it would appear that you have met by chance, no blame will attach to your actions, and you may be able to resolve the misunderstanding and mend the relationship. In your communication with the other person, be sure that you speak your truth, and that your words are clear and direct. Make every effort to correct any aspect of miscommunication, for if there is clarity between you, all will be well.

LINE 3: If you make any attempt to heal the alienation that exists between you and another person or group, you will find yourself checked, possibly forcefully, and this will lead to humiliation. Do not be disheartened by your failure to resolve the misunderstanding. In the end, the relationship will survive and thrive, and all will go well. You may receive help from a friend or from a person in authority. Look for that person and see if you can enlist his or her aid.

LINE 4: You are enmeshed in an alienated situation and lack the resources to resolve it. However, you may receive help from a person from whom you would not ordinarily expect it. Look for that person, and you will find, to your surprise, that he or she shares your view of the situation. You will not incur any blame for your actions.

LINE 5: You are in a position of leadership but lack the resources and knowledge to resolve the general condition of alienation that now prevails. However, you can overcome it by asking for help from one or two people who are close to you or to the situation. Due to certain conditions, they are restrained from taking the initiative in coming to your aid, but, if you invite them to approach you, they will overcome the restraints and help you to put an end to this time of alienation. All feelings of remorse or regret will pass by.

TOP LINE: You have come to believe that some friends or associates are behind the alienation, but you have misjudged them, and your misconceptions are hurtful to all. Your first inclination is, or was, to punish them by hurting them. However, if you see that you were wrong, you will find that they are your true friends and allies. The misunderstanding will be cleared up, the tensions will ease, and good fortune will come.

39
CHIEN

Dangerous Adversity

THE KUA

If you continue on your chosen course of action at this time, you will place yourself in the path of dangerous adversity. Do not confront the danger. Instead, make a cautious retreat, and then develop a different course of action. Be sure to consult the oracle again regarding the new plan before putting it into effect. If you proceed in that way, all occasions for remorse will disappear, and in small matters, you will achieve good fortune. You are acquainted with a qualified person who can offer you useful guidance that will allow you to see a way out of the danger. Your retreat is only temporary, and if you persist in a new course of action and act prudently, you will triumph in the end. To retreat does not mean to give up the battle. On the contrary, retreating preserves resources and allows time to regain strength, renew forces, and make new plans. Thus, retreat makes possible a countermovement, which makes possible your success. Remain true to what is highest and best within you.

In general, opposition appears as obstruction, but superior persons use it to their advantage. They use opposition or obstructions to gather strength, cultivate their character, and plan a more productive course of action. Inferior persons, ignorant of the laws of the Universe, react to opposition by bemoaning their fate, blaming circumstances or other people, and giving up in their attempt to reach their goals.

THE LINES

BOTTOM LINE: You lack the strength and resources to overcome the adversity that lies ahead, and there is no one to whom you can turn for help. If you persist in pursuing your goal, you will encounter ever-greater difficulties and danger. A cautious retreat is the safest and most appropriate course of action at this time. Be assured that this time of dangerous adversity will pass and that you will again make progress. During this time of waiting, examine the situation carefully and plan how you will proceed after this time of dangerous adversity has passed. Once you have developed a new plan to achieve your goal, consult the oracle again to learn whether it will bring you the success you seek. Keep in mind that the present circumstances, which have resulted in your having to pull back temporarily, are for your complete benefit and will ultimately work to your advantage. If you adopt that frame of mind, you will not waste this time of waiting in empty hoping but will occupy yourself with useful preparations for the time when you will be able to move ahead again.

LINE 2: You are encountering dangerous adversity, and it seems as though the wise choice would be to retreat, but because it is your responsibility to another to move forward, you should do so. Even though you may believe that you lack the strength or resources to confront this danger, go forward anyway, and face it to the best of your ability. Ultimately, you will achieve success and earn the goodwill and respect of everyone around you. Even though danger threatens, you will be safe because you are fulfilling your duty to another, for which you will be held blameless.

LINE 3: If you continue in your present course of action, you will be faced with dangerous adversity that is impossible for you to overcome. Prudence demands that you not march ahead into certain defeat. Turn back, and your friends, associates and family will welcome you. When confronted with such overpowering forces, the safest and most appropriate course of action is to retreat. That does not mean that you have suffered a defeat, but rather that you are regrouping and developing a new plan for moving forward after the dangerous adversity has passed.

Be sure to consult the oracle again regarding your new plan before putting it into effect.

LINE 4: You lack the strength and resources to overcome the dangerous adversity that lies ahead. Retreating will lead you to allies who will assist you in overcoming this adversity. After you have recruited the help you need and have developed a new plan, consult the oracle again to see if it will lead you to the success you seek.

LINE 5: You are surrounded by dangerous adversity. However, because you are a superior person of integrity, loyalty, and honor, friends will come to your aid, and this will lead to success.

Do not proceed without help, because you are not equal to the task at this time. After you have found your helpers and developed your plan, consult the oracle again to make certain that it is a good one. By proceeding in that manner, your endeavor will succeed, and you will be blessed with good fortune.

TOP LINE: During this time of dangerous adversity, you may be called upon to help in some way. Although you are outside the situation, do not shirk your responsibilities. Instead, go forward and lend all the assistance you can. You may appear to lack the strength and resources to overcome the impending adversity, but, if you meet it and lend your assistance, you will get help from someone in authority. Also, your courageous action will earn you great merit and recognition.

40
HSIEH

Abatement of Danger

THE KUA

The danger subsides. If your question concerns the taking of action, taking that action will cause the danger to completely dissipate, thus bringing you good fortune. Reflect carefully on the entire situation related to your question. If you need to take any further steps to finish abating the danger, attend to those immediately so that there will be no chance of it recurring. Avoid spending too much time deliberating. Once you have considered any matter carefully, anxious hesitation will only cause you to miss your opportunity, for too much reflection cripples the power of decision. After you have reduced or eliminated the danger, return to your normal actions and conditions as quickly as possible. Only take whatever actions are necessary to reduce or eliminate the danger.

To reduce or eliminate the danger that threatens, resolve any open conflicts, settle any existing arguments, forgive mistakes, and pardon even intentional violations. Such actions will lessen any remaining tensions and pave the way for a return to normal conditions. After the danger has completely subsided, you may feel so relieved that you want to celebrate. That is natural, but avoid letting yourself be carried away, for that will work against you. By quickly taking the actions necessary to abate the danger, you will have good fortune.

THE LINES

BOTTOM LINE: The danger is beginning to lessen and will soon be gone. The only action you should take is to continue on the path to achieving your goal and make certain that your actions are in accord with the highest standards of integrity. If you persevere on that path, the danger will subside completely, and you will achieve success and meet your goal.

LINE 2: Several obstacles still block you from eliminating the danger, but you are in a strong position and capable of attending to them yourself, even though you can call on a person in authority for help if you need it. At all costs, avoid taking any rash or extreme action, for that will only heighten the danger. If you continue to behave with dignity and moderation, while also upholding the highest standards of integrity, you will meet with good fortune.

LINE 3: There is an indication that you are making a show of your wealth or position. That never works to your advantage. If you persist, you will heighten the danger rather than reducing or eliminating it. In this time when danger can be abated, it is crucial that you remain modest and unassuming, and avoid any display of your wealth or position, for that will attract envy on the part of others. Remember that the Universe favors the modest and undermines the arrogant. Returning to your former modest ways will bring you success and will reduce or eliminate the danger.

LINE 4: You are being loyal to an associate or friend who is of undesirable character or of low position. Even though the danger is diminishing, to eliminate it completely, you will have to sever your relationship with that person of low character or position to whom you have been loyal. You may feel some sadness over having to terminate your connection with that person, but you must do it. Once you do, another friend or associate will come to your aid. You can and should rely on that person.

LINE 5: You are in a position of leadership, and it is your responsibility to eliminate a danger that threatens you, but you are associated with inferior people who are causing the danger. You will not be able to succeed in eliminating the danger unless you break with them. Trust and rely on your own judgment, and take the action necessary to sever your relationship with them. You will then succeed in eliminating the danger, and good fortune will come to you.

TOP LINE: Danger from an inferior person threatens you. To eliminate the danger you must sever your relationship with that person. Study your situation, and try to discern whether you are involved with a person whose ideals and motives are not as elevated as your own. Once you identify that person, you must rid yourself of his or her influence. It is always necessary to choose friendships and close relationships with the utmost care, for certain people will uplift you and give you strength, while others will pull you down and sap your energy. Good friends are an eternal blessing, but bad relationships can potentially ruin your entire life. If you follow the path of the superior person, you will naturally choose only friends and associates who are superior persons themselves.

41
SUN

Decrease

THE KUA

This is a time of decrease when the topic of your question is decreasing or is about to decrease. If your question was with regard to the taking of action, taking the action will bring about decrease and therefore should be avoided. If your question is about an existing situation, know that it is or soon will be in a time of decrease. During this time, restrain your anger so that arguments or difficulties will not arise that will further the decrease. During this time of decrease, remain modest and sincere and avoid any outward displays of wealth. Only small accomplishments can be made at this time. Since this is a condition of the time, it will pass away of its own accord. What is important is that you act in accord with this time, attempting only the achievement of lesser goals. Regarding financial matters, security and happiness prevail when you keep income and expenditures in balance. Because all periods of prosperity are followed by periods of decline, the superior person uses prosperous times to prepare for times of decline.

If you pretend abundance when you are actually in need, those who could help you will not, either because they believe your pretense of abundance, or because they see through your pretense and therefore find you undeserving. Furthermore, if you pretend to have something when you do not, you will destroy your self-respect.

At this time, you will benefit by undertaking a project as well as maintaining the utmost integrity. Take neither gain nor loss to heart. You are not your gain; neither are you your loss. What is important is your reverence for All-That-Is, and your personal philosophy that you are a golden child of an indestructible Universe where everything that happens benefits you. Having that personal philosophy permits you to maintain happiness in the face of decrease. The decrease that you are now experiencing or will soon experience is only a phase that will soon turn to a time of increase. What matters is that, during this time of decrease, you seek to improve yourself in whatever ways you can, so that when this time of decrease is over, you will be prepared to take advantage of the time of increase and will thereby maximize its full potential.

This time of decrease is great indeed and brings good fortune to you, but only if you use your time effectively to prepare for the time of increase that always follows. Remember, the ancient text advises you to undertake a project at this time.

THE LINES

BOTTOM LINE: At this time, attend first to your own affairs, but then turn your attention to helping those in need. Go quickly to their aid, but also depart quickly after you have completed your task without boasting about or taking any credit for your actions. Also, weigh carefully how much you can afford to draw on your own resources to benefit others, just as persons who are receiving help must weigh how much they can receive without hurting you or themselves. If you are in need and are receiving help from another, weigh how much help you can accept without hurting the person who is helping you.

LINE 2: You are strong and in a key position. Despite this time of decrease, you will be safe, provided that you continue to follow the path of utmost integrity and refrain from undertaking any new projects. If you see an opportunity to help someone without weakening your own assets or position excessively, do so, for it will bring you good fortune.

LINE 3: You may lose a friend or helper due to some difficulty that may arise. If that happens, do not be concerned, for it is meant to happen, and whatever is meant to happen always brings a benefit. If you are working or traveling alone, you will find a companion. That also will work to your benefit. Where three people are working or traveling together, usually one of them will leave the group. Do not be concerned because that is to be expected.

LINE 4: There is an indication that you have character defects that are keeping you from reaching your goals and achieving success. In this time of general decrease, you will find it easy to mend these flaws. Then your friends and associates will come to you and offer their help. If you have not already done so, study the section on "The Superior Person" on page 387, and compare your own character traits with those listed. Make those character traits your own for they will lead you to a life of success and good fortune.

LINE 5: Although this is a time of decrease, you will be greatly increased by moving forward to the accomplishment of your goal. You may move confidently forward because your success is decreed from on high, and no one can stand in your way. Move forward in the knowledge that you will be successful, and act with the utmost integrity. Then, when you achieve your success, you will be able to enjoy it rather than feeling bad because you obtained it dishonestly. If you act with honor, supreme good fortune will be yours.

TOP LINE: In this time of decrease, you either find yourself able to help others without overly diminishing your own assets and resources, or you are able to bring increase to yourself without overly diminishing others' assets and resources. There is no blame in either action. You will benefit from continuing to follow the path of utmost integrity, for that will bring you good fortune. You will also benefit from undertaking a project at this time. Because of your unfailing ethical behavior, you will be blessed with many helpers.

4 2
I

Increase

THE KUA

This is a time of increase when you will prosper and find
increase in the topic of your question. Such times inspire
awe and wonder because you cannot help but be aware of
the ways in which the Universe is benefiting you. Your plans
will be assisted, you will be helped to achieve your goals, and
your efforts will be rewarded with increase and gain.

However, for you to achieve these things, you must take
active steps to accomplish your goal. You cannot sit back and
wait for success to drop into your lap. In this time of increase,
you will be benefited by far-reaching ideas. Keep in mind
that, if the increase and gain of this time are to be great, they
must benefit others as well as yourself.

The ancient text also states that when you see good in
another, you should imitate it, and when you find faults

within yourself, you should correct them immediately. Those are two of the most important character attributes you can cultivate, and persevering in them will lead to great good fortune and success.

Furthermore, if you persevere along that path, even among the lucky, you will stand out as the chosen one. During this time of increase and gain, you must remain true to the highest principles of ethics and integrity. Then you will enjoy your increase and gain once you have attained it.

THE LINES

BOTTOM LINE: This line indicates that you will receive help from the Universe itself. With the energy, strength and resources you receive from on high, you will be able to accomplish great goals that would ordinarily be out of your reach. Obstacles will be swept out of your way, and your progress will be like that of an eagle soaring in flight. Here at the beginning, you have the strength and resources to immediately advance toward accomplishing your goals. You can also obtain help from a well-positioned person in authority if you need it. Remain true to the highest moral and ethical standards so you will be able to enjoy your goals once you attain them. If you continue to act in accordance with what is highest and best within you, you will be rewarded with supreme good fortune.

LINE 2: This line says that you will receive the support of the Universe in reaching your goal. Your duty is to cultivate and strengthen your character for achieving this great success, namely by adhering to the highest moral and ethical intentions and behavior. Then, because of Universal law, your goal will come about naturally. You may find yourself receiving help from an unexpected or outside source. If you do, remember that this help is a gift from the Universe, and be sure to acknowledge not only the person who has brought you the help but also the Universe itself. You will benefit even more if your goals also help others as well as yourself, because your conduct will be in harmony with Universal law. Your success will then be great, not just in terms of magnitude, but also in terms of quality. Even the spiritual realm will heap blessings upon you.

LINE 3: A seemingly unfortunate event will befall you, but because this is a time of gain and increase, it too will bring you enrichment. That event will only appear unfortunate because, at the outset, you may not see the benefit that it will ultimately bring. In human life, some people will see a particular event as a benefit while others will see the same event as misfortune. However, enlightened persons who have walked through the fire of life and learned from it, have found that misfortune, loss, and adversity are ultimately fictions, and that every event, no matter how dire it may appear, is, in fact, a gift and for our total benefit. One of the goals of our journey through life is to discover that the ultimate nature of the Universe is that it is loving. Once we learn that, we know that everything that occurs is for our benefit, even when we are in the grip of calamity, terrible loss, or extreme adversity. When we act in accord with what we know, reality shapes itself accordingly. Even the flowers, the stones, and the animals know us as we pass by when we have attained that level of awareness. If you conduct yourself with modesty and integrity, follow the path of moderation, and show those in authority that you deserve your enrichment, no one will criticize you or find fault with you.

LINE 4: You are in an excellent position because you are close to those in authority and you enjoy the support of your subordinates. You can be of great service at this time by acting as an intermediary between the two groups. Do not act out of selfish motives, but use your resources to benefit all concerned. If you avoid extremes and show loyalty to those in authority, they will be inspired to follow your lead and will entrust you with great responsibility. Do not take all the credit, but share it with others.

LINE 5: In this time of increase and gain, you have distinguished yourself by the complete integrity of your intentions and actions. Although these are their own reward, the generous and loving Universe also recognizes your excellent character attributes and will now reward you. You are strong and in a position of leadership, and you enjoy the support of those under you. Remember, in this time of increase, to help and support them and anyone else for whom you are responsible. Your kindheartedness will earn you the respect and even love of everyone around you, and you will enjoy supreme good fortune.

TOP LINE: You have amassed wealth, position, and influence for yourself but have failed to distribute any of it to those below you. This self-serving and thoughtless behavior will bring you misfortune. Act as quickly as you can to remedy this situation and to distribute some of your abundance to those worthy people who need help. Also assist them with your position of influence. In this way, you may succeed in minimizing the negative consequences of your selfish behavior.

43
KUAI

Overthrow of the Dark Force

THE KUA

The five strong, solid, light-giving lines in this kua represent you and your allies, or you working alone. Whichever is the case, the lines are an unstoppable force that will mount upward and overthrow the broken top line, which usually represents an evil person, a group, a destructive habit, a disruptive family member, an opposition faction within a group, or some other dark entity. Although the dark force represented by the top line appears weak, it is not. Its dark force destroys and undermines slowly and treacherously, and because it is at the top of the kua, it is powerful and in a controlling position.

The situation is dangerous, and you must take great care in dealing with this force, whatever or whoever it is. The ultimate outcome is not in doubt because the five lower lines are far too strong to be stopped by the one weak, broken line at the top. However, the overthrow must be accomplished in the right way because, if you resort to evil methods, you will become an ally and an instrument of evil, and the overthrow will become that much more difficult. It is a Universal law that evil or dishonest tactics will always rebound against you. If you continue to follow the path of utmost integrity, you will not give the dark force any weapons to use against you. Under no circumstances should you resort to force, for that too will only work against you. The most powerful way to fight evil is always to do good. The evil entity must be openly discredited and denounced, and everyone involved or affected by the overthrow must be informed of the plan. Finally, your overthrow must be complete, or else the dark force will rise again to cause harm to you and to those around you.

During times when dark forces are being overthrown, you should help those below you with your resources and assistance. To provide that assistance now will benefit you. Nor should you be content with yesterday's honors, but you should constantly press on to ever-greater achievements. It will benefit you at this time to undertake a project. If you follow the counsel offered here, you will succeed in overthrowing the dark force, and great acclaim and rewards will be yours.

THE LINES

BOTTOM LINE: You are strong and eager to overthrow the dark force, but there is a strong indication that this is the wrong time to take such action, or that you are not up to the task at this time. If you proceed now, and try to completely overthrow the dark force, you will most likely fail. Assess your strength and resources to determine whether they are adequate to the task. If you have help or allies, take those strengths and resources into account as well, but success is still unlikely at this time. Initiating action from a position of any weakness whatsoever will expose you not only to failure but also a serious setback. Make no attempt to proceed past what you know to be the point of certain success, because any great attempt to completely overthrow the evil element will meet with misfortune. If you make any attempt at all, be sure it is extremely modest.

LINE 2: The most important guidance of this line is caution and preparation. While you are in the midst of planning to overcome the dark force, a sudden and alarming disruption occurs. Do not lose heart, for there is no reason for you to fear anything in this situation. You have the strength and resources to proceed, but you should be cautious. If friends or associates are helping you, alert them to the danger and urge them to be cautious as well. It is essential that you remain alert at all times because the danger is definitely present in the situation. Although the dark force may appear weak, it is actually powerful, so remain on your guard, and then you will have nothing to fear.

LINE 3: You are strong, courageous, and determined to do your part in overthrowing the dark force. However, the moment to conquer it is not yet at hand. Until then, make no attempt to break off your relationship with the dark force, for it will retaliate, and you are not in a position to withstand such retaliation, and your cause will be lost. Unfortunately, your allies and associates will misunderstand your continuing your relationship with the dark element, and they may turn away from you, leaving you to continue your undercover battle alone. That will be difficult for you, but persevere in your course of action, and later they will see that you had not changed your intentions to overthrow the dark force, but that you continued to do your part. At that point, they will apologize, and all will be well. In the end, no one will have any reason to hold anything against you because you will have been relentless in your determination to overthrow the evil force.

LINE 4: Do not insist stubbornly on trying to complete the overthrow of the dark force on your own, because it is not possible. Any attempt to do so at this time will only expose you to danger, and you will find it difficult, if not impossible, to make any progress. If you give up your effort to act as an individual and instead join with others of like mind and purpose, all cause for regret will vanish. You know someone who can offer you good counsel about how to conquer the dark force. Find out who that person is and ask for help because that will lead to success. However, the ancient text states that you will probably not follow that advice because of your stubbornness.

LINE 5: You are obligated to demonstrate unflinching resolve in overthrowing the dark force because you are in the leadership position and must set an example for those who are following you. Besides conquering the dark force itself, you must also overthrow all the other dark forces associated with it, or they will spring back again. Although your determination at this time must be unshakable, you must also avoid extreme measures of any kind and persevere in following only an ethical and moral course of action. You are likely to experience setbacks, but you must persevere to the end. Do not be discouraged by failure. There can be no half-victories here, for this is an all-or-nothing battle.

TOP LINE: We must weed out evil completely if it is not to spring up again. The best way to accomplish this is to hold completely to what is good. To stray even slightly from the path of the superior person is to start on the path of the inferior person, and that can lead only to misfortune.

This is the line that represents the evil force that the five lower solid lines are attempting to overthrow. The person, process, entity, or force is thoroughly evil, so show it no mercy, no matter how much it pleads, for, given the least opportunity, it will spring back again. You must conquer and overthrow it and any evil forces associated with it, if you are to achieve and maintain success. After the evil force has been completely overthrown, you must be on a constant lookout for the slightest sign of it coming back again. It is precisely at the moment of victory that we must be most cautious. Nothing is easier than to become thoughtless and easygoing at the point of success, so remain vigilant.

44
KOU

Return of the Dark Force

THE KUA

In this kua, the dark force returns suddenly and unexpectedly. No matter what its form, whether as a malicious or evil-minded person or as a temptation or an influence, it will in some way be a bad influence and cause harm.

If the dark force is a woman, she has great power, even though she appears gentle and weak. Be careful and do not ally or associate with her in any way, however unthreatening and alluring she appears.

She will use her harmless appearance to tempt you into dropping your defenses so she can seize control of the situation and cause you great harm.

If the dark force is a man, he may appear good-natured and harmless, but he is not. On the contrary, he is powerful and bent on bringing harm to you and those in your circle. Do not give him any power or associate with him in any way whatsoever. Do not be deluded into thinking that, because he appears harmless, you can safely spend time with him, because that is how he obtains influence and finds opportunities to cause you harm. Resist him from the outset.

This is a dangerous time for you and for everyone around you. To counteract the dark force, you should develop a plan to protect yourself, your family, group, or organization. Alert everyone about the dark force and warn them of its potential for harm. Take appropriate steps and precautions to neutralize the danger in this crucial time. If the dark force gains even a toehold, it will quickly grow to alarming proportions. It will be to your advantage to begin a project at this time.

THE LINES

BOTTOM LINE: The dark force has just begun to take hold. You must stop it immediately before it gains power and becomes too strong to overcome. If you fail in that effort, misfortune will result. Although the force may appear harmless, it is not and will cause great damage. You have the opportunity, here at the beginning, before it has gained an advantage, to identify it, to make those around you aware of it, and to stop it. Do not resort to force. Continue as always to follow the path of utmost integrity, but take effective action. If you act promptly and decisively, you and all those around you will be safe. After you have identified and conquered the dark force, remain on your guard to prevent its resurgence.

LINE 2: A prize or treasure is attracting the dark force, but you have the strength, resources, and position to oppose it, and you must do so to prevent it from contaminating those around you. Avoid any use of force, and continue to follow the path of utmost integrity, but do not relax your efforts until the dark force has been vanquished completely. You need not display hostility to it, as hostility might actually work against you, but you must maintain a complete resolve to stop the dark force before it becomes too strong for you to overcome.

LINE 3: An alluring yet dangerous temptation presents itself, but fortunately, you are prevented from indulging in your desire to yield to it. Something or someone is keeping you from forming a relationship with the dark force. That person or force is completely beneficial to you and should not be interfered with in any way. If you remain aware of the danger and keep yourself from giving in to the temptation, all will be well. If you yield to the temptation to associate with the dark force, great misfortune will come to you.

LINE 4: In this time when the dark force is returning, you are in a trusted position of authority, but you have neglected to maintain a good relationship with your subordinates. Take whatever steps are necessary to correct that situation as quickly as possible, for they will be of enormous value to you in combating the dark force.

Resist any temptation to associate with the dark force, however harmless and unthreatening it may appear, for it will cause great harm to you and to those around you if it gains any power. Renew and maintain your good relationships with your subordinates, and all will be well. If you fail to do so, you will incur misfortune.

LINE 5: You have the strength, resources, and position to protect those around you from the dark force that now threatens. If you do so in a low-key, unassuming way, you will reap great rewards for yourself and for those under your protection. Your associates are trustworthy, and if you place your trust in them and give them the freedom to follow their own guidance, they will not disappoint you, and they will help you by preventing the dark force from gaining influence and power. They will also continue to be loyal to you.

TOP LINE: However much you try to avoid meeting with the dark force, you will fail. If you are overly aggressive and hostile when that encounter takes place, it will lead to humiliation. Your decision to remain apart from the dark force must be unshakeable, but avoid excessive forcefulness. Live up to your good intentions and avoid anything other than minimal contact with the dark force. If you do, no harm will come to you or to your associates. There may be petty gossip from people in the community or maybe even your associates because they are jealous of your position, but they cannot harm you in any way.

45
TS'UI

Gathering Together, Joining

THE KUA

This is a time when you can either join a group or gather others into a group. If you are joining a group, you should have a clear understanding of why you are joining and what you hope to accomplish. The group will have its own goals and reasons for its existence, but you must be clear about your own personal goal or what you want to obtain for yourself by joining. If you are creating a group, you must have a well-defined cause that will draw all the members together and earn their support. To attract followers, you must be enthusiastic about your goal, so that you will gain their interest and ignite their own enthusiasm. The goal must be meaningful and worthwhile, or your members will soon drop out.

Being the leader of a group requires sincerity, strength, and dedication to the group's well-being. Your motives for creating a group must be ethical, moral, and rooted in an inner desire not just to meet your own needs but to be of service to the members and to those outside the group. There is some indication that you can gain valuable information about your undertaking by seeking advice from a qualified person before you begin. Once you define your goal and develop clear-cut guidelines for achieving it, you must always move in the direction of your goal. Your followers will rely on you to set an example, so you will have to show them that you are tireless, dedicated, enthusiastic, and loyal.

Whether you are joining or creating a group, choose your associates with great care. Universal forces are at work bringing together those who belong together. At this time, the Universal forces may bring people to you who may not be to your personal liking but who nonetheless will be of great benefit to you or to the group. According to the ancient text, you should remain open-minded when you are either talking with members of a group you are considering joining or talking with potential members of the group you are forming. You need not concern yourself about finding the right people, for they will come. The ancient text also states that you can obtain good fortune by making a great offering. The ancient text urges you to prepare for the unexpected and to take whatever precautions you can to ward off any dangers that might arise. You will be called upon to make sacrifices to obtain your goal. Making sacrifices is appropriate. Success will be yours.

THE LINES

BOTTOM LINE: If you are creating a group, there is some indecision in your followers. Identify the source of their indecision, and take immediate steps to reassure them. They are lacking in strong leadership, so you must reach out to those who are wavering and offer them your confidence and strength. Renew their dedication to the achievement of the group's goal. You may need to offer them some kind of incentive or reward. If you are joining a group, your commitment to joining is weak, and your associates are adversely influencing you. If you seek guidance from a dedicated and highly placed member, all will be well, and you will not regret joining.

LINE 2: You are drawn to a person in authority who is strongly influencing you to join with him or her or a group. If you yield to that influence, good fortune will come to you. After joining, you will enhance your position if you offer the group or its leaders something of value, such as a small gift or a commitment of time or resources. Your success is assured, and recruiting others to join will enhance your value and standing.

LINE 3: You would like to join with a person or a group, but you are receiving neither help nor encouragement. There may even be resistance to your joining. It is understandable that you would feel resentment or distress about such treatment, but if you take the initiative and find a key member of the group who can help you join, you will succeed, and those in authority will soon forgive you. Persevere and do not give up. Be confident, for this line indicates that you will be successful in the end.

LINE 4: You are responsible for recruiting people into the group. Doing so will bring you recognition and advancement, but it may also arouse resentment on the part of other members who envy your success. Because you are well motivated and intelligent and have the group's best interests at heart, you make the wise choice to remain modest and unassuming and to give all the credit to those in authority. This gesture makes it impossible for anyone to accuse you of selfishness and results in great good fortune for you.

LINE 5: Whether you are the leader or a member of the group, you are in a key position to gather the other members together, and many will join you. Others will hesitate, but if you maintain your sincerity, honorable motives, and high ideals, you will eventually win them over, and all will be well. This period calls for perseverance and patience above all. You must show your strength and dedication to the group and to the achievement of its goals, for you will be the central figure around which the group will rally.

TOP LINE: You have waited too long to join, and now you have lost your opportunity. You regret this deeply, but you still have a chance of succeeding if you go to the person or people you wish to join and make them aware, with all the respect due to them, that you regret not having joined earlier. Do not act forcefully or assertively, for those behaviors will work against you. If you demonstrate that you are dedicated, sincere, and persistent, all will be well.

46
SHÊNG

Advance

THE KUA

This is a time for advance, which will bring supreme success. You will find that your advance will be unobstructed. Even the greatest and most difficult goals can be achieved if we break them down into simple, easy steps.

For example, we may have trouble envisioning an entire year, but if we divide it into months, then days, and then hours, it stops feeling overwhelming.

To contemplate an entire trek up a great mountain is daunting; however, one step up the mountain is easy to take, and so follow the rest of the steps until the summit is reached. Instead of feeling discouraged or overwhelmed, it is best to divide great goals into small, easily handled tasks that we can carry out one step at a time. Do not waste energy thinking about the outcome. Simply begin and then continue to the end, one step at a time.

During this time of action, it is essential that you seek help and guidance from a qualified person. You need not be fearful, for a successful outcome is certain. Being loyal and devoted will benefit you. If you continue to follow the path of utmost integrity, you will rise to great heights of achievement and you will be recognized for your accomplishments.

THE LINES

BOTTOM LINE: You are just beginning the forceful advance called for at this time. This beginning will demand all your patience and power if it is to lead to a prosperous and successful ending.

You are starting from a weak position because you lack certain resources, but even insignificant power can result in great success if used effectively. To use what power you have effectively, you must first fix the goal firmly in your mind so that you see it clearly and imagine yourself attaining it. Then commit yourself to reaching it. Finally, use the power at your disposal to advance constantly in the direction of your goal by seizing every opportunity and turning it to your benefit. Just as dripping water wears away the hardest rock, never let your perseverance slacken, and you will eventually reach your goal. Because you will accomplish your goal despite your relative lack of power and resources, this achievement will earn you great respect, great good fortune, and success. Your power will blossom, and you will go on to other, even greater, deeds. If you obtain the trust and confidence of people of influence, you will benefit greatly and bring great good fortune to them as well as to yourself.

LINE 2: You possess great strength and resources and are in a favorable position to make an advance. Those in authority support your plans. Be sincere in your actions and put all your efforts toward reaching your goal. Then your advance will go smoothly, and no one will have grounds for criticizing you. Avoid confusing power with extreme measures. You must move forward by relying on your own ceaseless efforts, not on extreme measures. If you call upon the leader for help, he or she will not refuse you. Remember to act with the utmost courtesy and only along socially accepted paths. At this time, it is proper for you to make a small offering or gift to show your sincerity. It is not the value of the gift that is important, but your sincerity in offering it. Your gift will be greatly appreciated.

LINE 3: You are in a strong position and have the resources to take a major step forward. Because you have the approval and support of those in authority, no obstacles will stand in the way of your progress. Move forward quickly, but be on your guard, because the lack of obstructions may lull you into an unwarranted sense of security that could become your undoing. Remain watchful and careful, and continue to follow the honorable path to your success.

LINE 4: You have distinguished yourself in the eyes of those in authority, and they will now honor you for your trustworthiness and loyalty. If you have not already done so, this is a time when your powerful advance can achieve the pinnacle of success.

You will enjoy good fortune, and no one will find fault with you or your actions. If you remain modest and unassuming, you can continue your successful advance. Furthermore, if you have carried out your mission while keeping the Universal principles of integrity, honor, and durability in mind, your success will be long lasting.

LINE 5: You are in a strong and influential position. Your goal is finally in sight, but you run the danger of letting your success go to your head. If you lose your focus or grow careless now, you may lose sight of crucial matters and thereby lose the goal that is so near. It is precisely when success is within your grasp that you must remain the most focused, clearheaded, cautious and sober.

By continuing to act as you have until now, you will reach your goal safely and surely. If you continue to be careful and meticulous, you will consolidate your position and go on to other great achievements. However, take care to advance slowly, and avoid reaching too high, or you will turn your success into failure. Attend to all matters that need attention.

TOP LINE: You have advanced as far as you can at this time. Now is a time for extreme caution and unremitting perseverance in following a path of high ethical and moral behavior, or you will turn your success into failure. When anything, even success, reaches its maximum potential, Universal law dictates that it will always transform into its opposite. Thus, if you carry your success too far, the highest rung on your ladder of success will be failure. To avoid succumbing to that law, be content with what you have achieved and remain unremittingly watchful.

47
K'UN

Oppression

THE KUA

This is a time of adversity and oppression. If your question is about taking action, taking the action will bring on oppression and adversity. If your question is about a condition or situation that already exists, follow the guidance that follows to achieve success.

Times of oppression and adversity can lead you to feel exhausted and depressed, but by taking the appropriate action, you can take every turn of events, no matter how dire, and out of them create good fortune. You should be so certain of your ability to turn adversity into good fortune that you will stake your very life on your conviction. Once you have developed yourself and formed your character, you will be tested in the fire of life. The fire of life is the Universal force that endlessly shapes and alters you until you come to realize who you are in relationship to the rest of the Universe and learn to act accordingly. Usually, the altering process takes the form of adversity, and, as far as outward appearances are concerned, may seem to be working against you, when actually it is working for you. To see each of those instances for what they are, opportunities for growth and improvement, is the way of the sage. Seeing them in that light will bring an amazing change in your outlook, for you will then see all obstacles and adversities as opportunities, and you will consequently lose your resentment of them.

THE LINES

BOTTOM LINE: You are at the beginning of the period of oppression and adversity but are sitting idly by while the situation around you deteriorates, as if you are a weak person who lacks any control over his or her fate. If you do not change that attitude immediately, the situation will worsen, and you will sink more deeply into your sorrow. Uselessly complaining about what has befallen you will bring you misfortune. You should be making every effort to take your fate into your own hands. Rouse yourself to action, seek help, ask for advice, and take steps to change the circumstances facing you. If you proceed in that manner, you will create success out of seeming misfortune.

LINE 2: The adversity is so upsetting to you that you are finding it difficult to eat or sleep, and neither friends nor associates are offering you any help. However, a person in a position of authority may appear, and you may get some assistance from that person.

The present situation that is causing the oppression may require you to sacrifice effort, time, or resources to overcome the obstacles. It will be to your benefit to be reverent at this time, as in all times. Do not undertake any projects at this time; just content yourself with overcoming the oppression that now threatens.

LINE 3: You are allowing yourself to believe that the situation is worse than it is, and you are therefore overreacting in a way that will only bring on additional adversity and misfortune. Your thoughts are clouding your judgment and impairing your clarity to the point that you will fail to recognize friends or helpers when they come. Do what you can to achieve a more optimistic outlook immediately.

LINE 4: Although you are in a secure situation, you still feel anxious and irrationally concerned that you will lose everything. You are embarrassed about those feelings, which also causes your more clear-sighted friends and associates to think less of you. You will achieve your goal in the end, so be more optimistic now.

LINE 5: You are in a position of leadership and would like to help those under you, but your superiors and your subordinates are causing problems for you, which makes it difficult for you to make progress. Even a trusted friend or associate is creating adversity for you at this time. Endure this period patiently, and eventually you will experience happiness. Being reverent toward all things will benefit you.

TOP LINE: This time of oppression is drawing to a close, but you have become so caught up in your past adversities and difficulties that you are failing to perceive the arrival of better times and are therefore failing to take appropriate action. If you take a fresh look at your situation and initiate positive action, good fortune will be yours.

48
CHING

The Well

THE KUA

"The Well" is the symbol of the unchangeable, inexhaustible abundance of the Universe. It is the spiritual source of nourishment and wisdom from which all can draw. As it applies to you, it represents a teaching or information that is either given to you or that you give to another. In every case, The Well is an inexhaustible, abundant supply of spiritual nourishment, wisdom, help, assets, resources, information, good counsel, and strength. Those who draw an insufficient amount from the source will experience misfortune.

Encourage others to draw from the source and to help one another in drawing from it. The Well also means union, or joining together. You may find it advantageous to join with the subject under consideration or to have the subject join with you.

THE LINES

BOTTOM LINE: The source is muddy. Therefore, it is of no use to anyone, and no one can draw on it. Its time of usefulness may be past. If you are the source under consideration here, this line indicates that you have allowed yourself to stagnate and therefore have become of no use to anyone, not even yourself.

You may also be associating with people who are bad influences, indulging in dishonorable behavior, or have adopted a negative outlook on life. If you keep to that path, others will lose interest in what happens to you, and you will be left alone. That would be a terrible waste of the precious life with which the generous and loving Universe has seen fit to endow you. If you have not already done so, study the section on "The Superior Person" on page 387 so you can gain insight into how you can remedy your situation. If the subject of this reading is something or someone other than you, the same interpretation applies in that its usefulness may have come to an end due to neglect. That does not mean it is not salvageable but that it needs refurbishing or rejuvenating.

LINE 2: You are available but are not joining with others of like mind to dispense your wisdom, knowledge, or assets. That is unfortunate because you are a pure soul from whom others could reap great benefits. If you take immediate steps to restore and revitalize yourself and make those people with whom you wish to join aware of your willingness to join with them, all will benefit. In the past, you have allowed your mind to deteriorate, you have associated with inferior people, and you have therefore ceased to be of value to yourself or to others. Now that you have had a change of heart, you should make everyone, including those in authority, aware of your renewal and good intentions.

LINE 3: You have been purified and yet no one makes use of you, which is sad. If those in authority were made aware of your usefulness, all would benefit. Do what you can to show the people with whom you want to join your sincerity, good intentions, and usefulness. That action will lead to success.

LINE 4: You are undergoing a time of purification. While you are revitalizing yourself, you may not be capable of offering others your wisdom, knowledge, or resources, but after you have recovered your strength, life energy, and wisdom, you will have far more to offer than before. This is a productive time for you, which will bring great rewards because it is always admirable to make yourself the best that you can.

LINE 5: Here, in the place of the leader, you are pure and your wisdom is readily available, so that everyone can be nourished. Congratulations. You are a person of wisdom and intelligence, and you stand ready to advise and help others. Good fortune will come to all concerned. You will find great benefit in joining with others of like mind at this time.

TOP LINE: You are a pure, dependable source that is readily available, so that everyone can draw from you without hindrance. This brings supreme good fortune to all. You will find great benefit in joining with others of like mind at this time.

49
KO

Achievement

THE KUA

The situation is reaching a point where you can achieve what you want and cause the people to see as you do. It will be to your benefit to prepare for this time which is coming. If you hope to achieve success, do not let your thinking be rigid and inflexible. Instead, rather make yourself aware of changing conditions, keep abreast of the times, and change with them. That is how you will see the right moment for action and make no mistake. The Universal law that provides for constant change is the only thing that does not change, so to remain inflexible when all else is changing is to invite disaster. Rigidity leads to failure, but flexibility leads to success. Nonetheless, it is equally crucial for your success that you set a firm course and that your character is steady enough that you do not give in to and follow every passing fad or trend.

When the time for action is at hand, you will inspire the confidence of those who will assist you in bringing the change about by maintaining a positive and enthusiastic attitude. Motivate everyone to support your cause so that they can get behind you and offer their help. During this period, you will find it easy to enlist helpers, and your enthusiasm will carry you and them through to the end. You must cultivate endurance if you hope to attain your goal. It is important to make a plan and follow it carefully. Also, to achieve the change, you must have the best interests of everyone at heart, for, if your goals are selfish, your plans will lack greatness and will therefore come to nothing. This time is great, but only greatness of spirit will achieve a great ending. If you persist in following the path of utmost integrity and greatheartedness, you will achieve supreme success. You and those around you will benefit from organizing and coordinating your schedules to prepare for the time that lies ahead.

THE LINES

BOTTOM LINE: You know how to achieve your goal, and you have the strength and resources you need to do it, but the time is not yet at hand. If you begin prematurely, you will fail in your attempt. In the near future, another time will come when you may move forward confidently, but that time is not now. While you bide your time, prepare yourself and make plans, but reveal them only to those you can trust. Conceal your plans from everyone else. Your goal must be to benefit others as well as yourself if it is to achieve true greatness. Again, avoid taking any action at this time.

LINE 2: The moment has arrived where you can achieve your goal. You have the strength and clarity to bring it about, and you also have the support of those in authority. Now is the moment to take action to achieve your goal. If you wish to succeed, however, you must have a carefully developed plan that will arouse enthusiasm in your helpers. You must also prepare yourself by adapting yourself to whatever the new situation will bring. Use your imagination. You will achieve splendid success and will win the support of those around you. Good fortune lies ahead.

LINE 3: You have the strength to achieve your goal, but to begin now will bring misfortune, and to continue will put you at serious risk. Although it may appear that the moment to bring about your goal has come, it is, in fact, the wrong time to begin. Factors unknown to you will cause you to fail if you act now.

However, if you wait for the right moment, which will come soon, you will achieve a great success. Take action only after you have studied the situation, not once but several times, contemplated the ways of bringing your goal to fruition, and have sounded out your supporters to make sure they are behind you. Then, when the right moment arrives, take action.

LINE 4: You are strong enough to bring about the contemplated change but must first convince those in power of your sincerity and competence. You will find this an easy task, and then you will be able to move forward with the certainty of achieving your goal, even if it is to completely change the way people think. To succeed, will require inner strength as well as outer resources and authority. Be sure that your cause is just, for, if it is not, your followers will be disappointed, and your success will turn to failure. Continue to follow the path of utmost integrity, and all will be well. Good fortune.

LINE 5: You are strong, in a position of leadership, and enjoy your followers' support. You inspire those around you, so the goals you achieve will benefit everyone. You will accomplish them brilliantly, but to ensure that you achieve your goals, you must make the guidelines clear to everyone. Be sure that each person involved has a clear picture of what the change will entail and knows what part he or she will play in achieving the goal.

TOP LINE: When superior persons makes corrective changes within themselves, the changes are deep and long-lasting, and they shine forth with brilliance and beauty. Inferior persons make short-lived, superficial changes, and only for effect. At this time, all the changes and goals necessary have been accomplished. You have come as far as you can, and, for now, it must be far enough. Your followers have also made all the changes possible for them, and although the changes may be superficial and may fall short of your hopes, you can expect nothing better at this time. Continue to follow the path of utmost integrity, for it will bring you good fortune. However, initiating further action now will bring misfortune.

5O
TING

The Cauldron

THE KUA

Ting is the symbol of the Cauldron, which dispenses spiritual wisdom and knowledge. This kua is formed of the two trigrams, Li, which represents intelligence and clarity, and Sun, which represents penetrating wind. Together, they symbolize the penetrating intelligence of a divine nature that is dispensed from the ting or cauldron.

This kua indicates either that you are a source from which spiritual wisdom is dispensed, or that the subject of your question will be a source of spiritual wisdom that will be dispensed to you and others. This kua brings supreme good fortune and success. However, to dispense great spiritual wisdom, you must first possess it, and to possess it, you must first seek it. Having found it, you will speak words of such wisdom that all people, both foolish and wise, will benefit from your presence. If you are called upon to dispense spiritual wisdom, it is only because you already possess it.

If you act with divine wisdom and intelligence, you will create a life of good fortune and success for yourself and for those around you. If your question concerns a project, pursuing it at this time will bring you great wisdom and will provide others with great wisdom. If your question concerns a person, he or she will either provide you with great spiritual wisdom, or you will provide him or her with it. If your question concerns a possible course of action, taking it will lead you to great spiritual wisdom. Receiving this kua in answer to your question means that moving forward will bring you supreme good fortune and success.

THE LINES

BOTTOM LINE: The Ting is upside down and is emptying its contents. That means that you are holding beliefs that conflict with the truth of your situation. You must metaphorically turn yourself upside down and empty those ideas from your mind. That emptying may require that you seek guidance from a person with whom you would not ordinarily associate, but no blame attaches to such action. This line also counsels you about how to succeed, for it states that even a small amount of power can result in success if used appropriately. To use what power you have effectively, you must first fix the goal firmly in your mind so that you see it clearly and imagine yourself attaining it. Then, commit yourself to reaching it. And finally, use the power at your disposal to advance constantly in the direction of your goal by seizing every opportunity and turning it to your advantage. Like the dripping water that wears away the hardest rock, never let your perseverance slacken, and you will eventually reach your goal. And because you will accomplish it despite your relative lack of power and resources, this achievement will earn you even greater respect.

LINE 2: You possess much spiritual knowledge and wisdom that will allow you to attain significant achievements. Because this is the kua of Ting, the Cauldron, your achievements should be directed at benefiting others as well as yourself. If your achievement can result in providing spiritual nourishment for yourself and others, your success will be that much greater. Your attainments may arouse some envy among your friends and associates, but they will not be able to harm you in any way. To lessen their envy, do not boast, and remain exceptionally modest. Good fortune will come to you.

LINE 3: You are strong but your position is weak and you are outside the circle of influential people, which causes you much sorrow. You could be of great benefit to them if only they knew of your capability, strength, and talent. The time is coming when you will be able to make an advance and carry out your good intentions to benefit the people, but first you must study the knowledge you will need for your advance by conversing with people who are experts in the field and reading books on the topic of your goal. When the time for your advance comes, you should give your wisdom freely so that people can use it for themselves. For that action, you will be greatly honored, you will see your influence grow and you will rise through the ranks. Remember to remain modest as you see your greatness come to fruition.

LINE 4: You are failing to use your best efforts to accomplish your goal. To succeed at this time will require great effort on your part coupled with unshakable determination. Do not give up, but advance. You would do well to seek out more reputable and honorable company. Pay particular heed to the remarks that the sage Confucius made regarding this line: "Weak character coupled with honored place, meager knowledge with large plans, and limited powers with heavy responsibility will seldom escape disaster." Unless you take a fresh look at the situation and approach it with great determination, you will suffer misfortune.

LINE 5: This line states that the Ting has gold handles and carrying rings, which means that you are in a position of leadership but have remained modest and approachable. This demonstrates a deep understanding of Universal law, and continuing those behaviors will benefit you. You may advance confidently toward achieving your goal. Because this is the kua of spiritual wisdom, you will benefit greatly if you endeavor in some way to spread your spiritual knowledge. You can now obtain strong and devoted helpers who will gather around you and support your undertakings. Although you are in the position of leadership, it is essential that you remain modest and share the credit for the goals attained.

TOP LINE: This line states that the Ting has jade carrying rings. Because jade is hard but has a soft sheen to it, this line means that you are strong and have risen to a position of prominence but continue to dispense spiritual wisdom and to help your friends and associates in their endeavors. If you continue this behavior, great good fortune and success will come to you, and everything you do will benefit you. Even the spiritual realm will heap blessings upon you.

51
CHÊN

Shock, The Arousing

THE KUA

Shock! A manifestation of the Universe. You have received or will receive a shock. Most people react to shock with fear and trembling, but superior persons do not let shock drive from their mind the constant awareness that they are divine creatures in a divine Universe, and that the shock was entirely for their benefit. For these reasons, they are always in a state of reverence and gratitude for All-That-Is. Only if you understand completely that the shock is entirely for your benefit will success come. If you react by complaining or bemoaning your fate, as if you have suffered a catastrophe, the true meaning of the shock will elude you, as will its blessings. All events, even those that cause us injury or deprive us of something, benefit us.

Disaster is a tap on the shoulder from the Universe, which brings about earthquakes, tornadoes, hurricanes, tidal waves, financial upsets, great losses, personal traumas, and emotional shocks as well as other terrifying situations and events. Such cataclysms remind us that the Universe is not only awe-inspiring but also sometimes terrifying. When such events occur, wise individuals are awed by them and use them as opportunities to examine their lives, to study whether their affairs are in order, and to reflect on whether they are living the life of the superior person. That is one of the great values of such events, for we can then order our lives according to the highest principles. The time of shock is truly great.

In this situation, if the shock has not yet arrived, and you want to prevent it from taking place, do not pursue the issue or matter in question further at this time. If you do decide to pursue it and the shock occurs, remember that it is a gift to you from the generous and loving Universe in which everything that happens benefits you and to the greatest extent possible.

THE LINES

BOTTOM LINE: You have experienced or will experience a shock or a traumatic event. It could take the form of a physical shock, an accident, a terrifying experience, a disaster, or alarming news. Whatever its form, you will be frightened at first. After the event is past, you will feel relieved, and eventually you will come to understand that the shock that caused you so much terror has actually brought you a great benefit that far outweighed the shock. If your question concerns taking action, to take the action will bring on the shock. To avoid the shock, do not take the action. Good fortune.

LINE 2: Shock comes to you and causes the loss of property, valuables, friends, or other things you treasure. Do not stop to try to save anything, but take immediate action to save yourself. Trying to combat the forces responsible for causing the shock will be useless. The ancient text says that after the time of shock passes, you will gain back all that you have lost. Therefore, there is no need to chase after your losses. Even as the shock overwhelms you, remember that it is a gift to you from the Universe.

LINE 3: Shock befalls you and frightens you. Shock often paralyzes us like deer caught in the headlights of a car, but if your fear spurs you to take action to escape the adversity, all will go well. If you do not take action, it will only lead to unfortunate consequences.

LINE 4: You are strong but surrounded by mediocre and disreputable people and are thus in an unfavorable situation. For this reason, when the shock comes, you feel as if you are stuck in quicksand and you cannot make a decisive move. You must rouse yourself to action and take whatever remedial steps you can to correct your situation.

LINE 5: You have received or will receive one shock after another. The situation holds some danger, but only if you panic. Do not lose your presence of mind. Remain calm, and do all you can to protect the people and prevent the loss of possessions. If you persevere, nothing at all will be lost.

TOP LINE: The shock has reached terrifying proportions, and everyone around you is so stunned and traumatized that they are unable to move. Avoid taking any action at this time. Let the time of shock pass. Some of your friends or associates, who are so terrified that they have rushed into action, will not understand why you are not doing the same. Do not follow their lead, for your proper course at this time is to remain calm and to not take any action except to wait for the shock to pass.

52
KÊN

Mountain, Stopping, Thoughts Coming to Rest

THE KUA

Universal law provides that every condition has a time for advancing or movement and a time for stopping or rest, and that each comes at its proper time. This is the time for stopping, so, with regard to your question, stop and take no further action at this time. To do otherwise will lead to misfortune. There are times when the best action is no action, and this is one of those times.

During this time of stopping, learn to quiet your heart and your inner being. Open yourself to the subtle inner promptings of the Universe, and know that everything is as it should be. The Universe is preparing the way for you to achieve what is in your best interests. Do not try to hurry this process, but be relaxed and confident. You have not been forgotten but are held at every moment in the great awareness. To achieve a quiet heart, rest and movement must follow each other in accordance with the demands of the time. If you have a quiet heart, you will be sensitive to the subtle promptings that come to you from the world around you, and this, in turn, will allow you to move effortlessly and smoothly through life, rather than blundering through it with great effort and difficulty. Acting in accord with the demands of the time always leads to harmony.

If you persist in remaining in motion during the time for rest, you will be unprepared when the time for action comes. On the other hand, if you remain still when the time for action comes, you will miss your opportunity, and what would have been easy to achieve will become difficult. The superior person first achieves a quiet heart, and then acts. Anyone who acts from these deep levels makes no mistakes. Meditation and concentration are good examples of trying to obtain by force what can be obtained only by calmness and relaxation. Using force will produce results opposite from those intended. Achieving inner composure first allows meditation and concentration to develop naturally and thereby produces the desired result. The symbol of this kua is the mountain. Be like the mountain: strong, stable, and still.

THE LINES

BOTTOM LINE: You are at the beginning. Stop. This is not the time for action. Calm yourself, develop your plans, and prepare for the time when you will be able to advance safely. When you believe that time is at hand, consult the oracle again to see whether you can safely advance.

LINE 2: A person in authority is urging you to join in an advance of some kind. You hold a minor position and are following the correct course in delaying action, but the person in authority, who may be the leader, plunges ahead into danger. You cannot prevent him or her from doing so, and, although you feel distress about the situation, you can do nothing about it. Do not allow yourself to be led astray by the leader. If anyone asks you to go against what you know to be right for yourself, the only correct action is to refuse. Do not do so in a disrespectful manner, because that will only earn you the displeasure of the person you are refusing. Instead, be respectful but firm. On the other hand, do not stubbornly refuse to ever pay attention to what a leader says or to good counsel from qualified persons. Rather, ask yourself if their course is best for you, and then make your own decision. In this case, take whatever action you can to protect yourself, and let the person in authority suffer the consequences of having made an untimely advance.

LINE 3: You are withholding your affection or love, or you are withholding a powerful desire or longing. Rigid and joyless self-denial are dangerous and unwholesome. Be gentler and less rigid with yourself. Life seeks to fulfill itself in joyous, vibrant expression, so allow yourself to be an instrument of life, and joy will follow.

LINE 4: You are nearing the attainment of your goals, but you have not yet attained calmness and peace. And for you, these are important goals that will lead to a state of well-being. Engage in practices that will allow calmness to arise within you. Learn to operate from your deep inner wells of understanding and intuition, and restrain your egotistical tendencies. Such discipline is difficult for everyone. It will be of particular benefit to you.

LINE 5: Because you are a leader, you must speak and behave in keeping with what is expected of people in your position. In particular, avoid any speech that might be considered offensive. Crude jokes, off-color comments, or sexually biased remarks diminish you in the eyes of others and can easily lead to a situation that you will regret. If you are reserved in your speech, your words will carry more weight. Keep in mind that sometimes the most eloquent statement is silence.

TOP LINE: This line indicates that you have attained a state of mind that is peaceful and at rest. If you maintain this tranquility and avoid any rash actions, you will be successful.

53
CHIEN

Gradual Development

THE KUA

This shows the process of gradual development, in which things develop slowly and, as a consequence, become strong and enduring. Because gradual development requires a long time, perseverance is required so that the develpment continues without ever stopping altogether.

The ancient text refers to the time when a maiden is given in marriage. It uses the flight of a wild goose as a symbol to depict the stages of development because the wild goose has only one mate in its lifetime and thus represents fidelity, trust, truthfulness, and loyalty—the essential attributes of every successful marriage, partnership, and relationship of any kind. No matter what close relationship is being formed, observing all the formalities in their proper order, just as a marriage proceeds from courtship to proposal to consummation, will bring success.

Gradual development pertains to all relationships or situations that are in the process of becoming established over time. Thoughtfulness, attention to detail, avoiding any violations of the bounds of social correctness, and never trying to hurry the development unnaturally will all bring success and good fortune. The object of your concern is in the process of gradual development and will thus progress slowly but continually, provided that you give it your attention. Similarly, if you are contemplating making a change in a relationship, carry it out gradually, not abruptly. It will be to your advantage to act with the utmost integrity during this time of gradual development, for that will set a good example for others. Also, during this time of gradual development, pay attention to the cultivation of your own character as well, for that is the key to a prosperous and peaceful future. Although attaining your goal may take a long time, you will enjoy lasting success and good fortune.

THE LINES

BOTTOM LINE: The process of gradual development is just beginning. As is true with all beginnings, great care must be taken if the planting is to lead to a harvesting. The ancient text uses the symbol of the wild goose just reaching the shore, which means that the situation is just starting to unfold. There is danger here, and no help is to be found. People may gossip about you, but they will not be able to harm you. The best defense against gossip is to live according to the highest standards of ethical and moral conduct at all times. If this is the beginning of a relationship, follow the guidance in the opening paragraph of the kua. You are fortunate because this line indicates that you will be successful. Be cautious, avoid hasty moves or rash actions, conduct yourself with modesty and honor, and you will meet not only with success, but also with good fortune.

LINE 2: Here, the ancient text speaks of the wild goose flying up to the top of the cliff, where it will find a safe resting place. The goose is not there yet, but the indication is that it will reach its goal. This means that the relationship has developed to the next stage, which is one of comparative safety. The relationship is not completely safe, but the progress has been good. You will benefit from establishing a cordial relationship with those in authority. At this time, it is appropriate for you to invite your friends and associates to gather and share in your success. However, because this is the time of gradual development and not yet the time of ultimate success, you must still press on. Good fortune awaits.

LINE 3: The ancient text states that the wild goose has landed on a dry and dusty plateau, which is not a safe or proper resting place. This means that you have exceeded the pace of gradual development and have left not only yourself but also others close to you open to danger. Your hasty actions have caused a conflict with someone in authority or with someone with whom you would like to join. You are in a vulnerable position, and others will seek to harm you or take advantage of you.

Resist them and press on to a place of greater safety. If your concern is about a relationship, those close to the other person will use their influence against you. Resist that as best you can. Your best defenses are your strong character and good intentions, so avoid provoking an argument with them or with the other person with whom you want to join. Instead, conduct yourself with the utmost integrity, loyalty, and forthrightness. Still, despite your good intentions this line indicates misfortune. By following the guidance given in this line, you will eventually overcome the adversity and all will go well.

LINE 4: The ancient text states that the wild goose has found a tree in which to rest. However, a tree is not a suitable resting place for a goose. The indication is that you have made gradual progress but are not yet in a compatible situation or relationship. It is important that you continue to move ahead, but carry out your gradual progress with gentleness, flexibility, loyalty, appropriate conduct, and perseverance.

LINE 5: The ancient text states that the wild goose is nearing the summit of the mountain. This means that you are nearing your goal, but there are still many obstacles to overcome. If you continue to use good sense, to live according to the highest moral and ethical values, and to remain persevering, you will eventually overcome the obstacles and meet with good fortune. You will find it easy to obtain important help from an influential subordinate.

TOP LINE: The ancient text states that the wild goose is flying up to the heavens. This means that the gradual development has surpassed the peak of success and is now an example to others. You are to be congratulated for the endurance and high ideals you displayed while pursuing your goal. You are a bright light, and everyone will recognize you as an example to be imitated. Because everything is so well ordered and the development has been so correct, continued good fortune is assured.

54
KUEI MEI

Entrance into or
Maintaining a Relationship

THE KUA

This kua depicts you in a difficult and unbalanced situation where you are either in a relationship or about to enter into a relationship of some kind. It could be a personal or love relationship, a partnership, a company, organization, a family, or any other type of group. In all cases, the situation is unfavorable because weak people have strong positions of influence and feel threatened by you. With regard to a personal or love relationship, maintaining it or entering into it requires that you be modest and gentle because aggressiveness on your part will arouse resentment and resistance either from the person with whom you want to have the relationship or those close to that person. Those close to the person will try to undermine you, either to protect the person from you or to protect their own relationship with that person. With regard to a group to which you already belong or which you would like to join, aggressiveness on your part will arouse resentment and resistance from some members. You must be able to fit yourself in smoothly without arousing anger, suspicion, fear, or distrust. Those already in the group are possessive of their positions and influence, and if you threaten them in any way, it will work to your disadvantage.

Relationships that are legally formed have a contract as a basis for conduct, but relationships based on voluntary participation require great tact and thoughtfulness if you are to successfully maintain or integrate yourself into the relationship or group. To be successful in your endeavor, you must exercise great caution, be willing to do more than your share, remain exceptionally modest, unobtrusive, friendly, open, and inviting, downplay your talent, good looks, and assets, and be careful not to threaten anyone's position. In that way, you will have the best chance of attaining your goal. However, it is a difficult situation. Neither good fortune nor misfortune is indicated by this kua because your success is entirely dependent on how you conduct yourself and how the members or the person receives you.

THE LINES

BOTTOM LINE: You have the strength and resources to move forward, but your position is weak, and you are only at the beginning of the situation. Therefore, you will have to accept a modest beginning in the relationship or a modest position in the family, organization or group, but if you behave correctly, you will be accepted. Make a plan, avoid harboring any hidden motives, continue to follow the path of utmost integrity, be modest, downplay your talent, assets, and good looks, let your good nature and outstanding character shine forth like beacons lighting your way, and move forward toward the attainment of your goal. Good fortune will be yours.

LINE 2: You are well positioned and have the necessary strength and resources to move forward. You have the support of the leader, who has maintained loyalty to you, but because the leader is weak, you will not receive much help. If you continue to maintain your loyalty to the leader who will then look to you for help and support, good fortune will be yours. You will be able to advance now without hindrance, but to be successful, you must advance without aggression while remaining modest, friendly, open, and true to that which is highest and best within you.

LINE 3: You are feeling and acting lighthearted because you have improved your status, but you lack the strength or resources to move forward on your own, and you also lack the support of those in power. The situation poses some danger because those in power are looking down on you for your unwarranted lightheartedness. You have the clarity and vision to understand this warning and to change your behavior.

LINE 4: You are strong enough and have the wish to move forward vigorously and joyously. Even though you lack the support of your subordinates at this time, you will be able to achieve your goal if you bide your time and wait for a favorable situation to develop. When you see that the situation has become more favorable, you may move forward.

LINE 5: You are in the leadership position and wish to move forward joyously and vigorously to the achievement of your goal while also benefiting others. You have the support of the leader and the support of your strong right-hand person. Because this is the time of vigorous, joyous movement, you may move forward with confidence because no one will hinder you. Good fortune lies ahead.

TOP LINE: The person or group with whom you want to join is not suitable for you. Any attempt to join with that person or group will meet with misfortune. You would do better to move on and look for someone else or another group.

55
FÊNG

Maximum Abundance

THE KUA

You have brought about or will bring about a time of maximum abundance. When anything reaches its maximum potential, it inevitably turns toward its opposite. Such changes are a product of the time and a function of Universal law, and there is no avoiding them. This is not to say that your abundance will not continue, but rather that you cannot increase it without running the risk of turning this time of abundance into a time of decrease. The best you can hope for is to prolong your abundance. Enjoy this time of success while it lasts. Resolve any unsettled disputes, and exact any unfulfilled penalties. This kua cautions you to remain modest and vigilant once you have acquired your treasure, whatever it is. Otherwise, the same Universal law that bestowed it upon you will remove it from you or cause it to work to your detriment. Do not delude yourself that your achievements, titles, and possessions are the totality or the be-all and end-all of life. They are merely the objects you have chosen to lead yourself along the path of life. Rather, it is the path itself that is the be-all and end-all of life, for it is on that path that you will learn the lessons of life and perfect yourself as a divine being in a perfect Universe.

THE LINES

BOTTOM LINE: Two people who both possess inner clarity and are capable of energetic action come together to preserve a time of abundance. They will both benefit if they spend enough time together to make a plan or accomplish a goal. There is no blame in this, and both people will benefit from the union. To move forward at this time will bring you recognition.

LINE 2: Inferior people are blocking and manipulating the person or group with whom you want to join. As a result, it has become almost impossible for you to form a relationship with that person or group. Any attempt on your part to advance or to establish a relationship with those in power will meet with distrust and suspicion. Your best course of action is to persevere in your sincerity, loyalty, good intentions and to continue your advance. In that way, you will eventually create trust and dispel the clouds that surround the situation, which will permit the union that you seek to come about. Good fortune will follow.

LINE 3: Inferior people have clouded the judgment of the person or group with whom you wish to join. As a result, you are unable to make progress at this time. You have suffered or will suffer an unfortunate and harmful turn of events. Take heart; it will ultimately work to your benefit. If you remain sincere and loyal, no blame will attach to you. Avoid any undertakings. Instead, bide your time for now until the moment comes when you can move forward again.

LINE 4: The general air of darkness is still present but has dissipated to some extent. You can now meet with another strong person who shares your viewpoint, and this meeting brings good fortune. Now you can move forward once again, and you should do so.

LINE 5: In this time of peak abundance, you are in a position of leadership but still remain modest and open. These qualities encourage strong, talented people to approach you and to offer their help. This in turn brings blessings, fame, and good fortune to all concerned, and prolongs the time of abundance.

TOP LINE: You have achieved great abundance, but this has caused you to become both arrogant and fearful of losing what you have. Your need to be master of the household or establishment has alienated you from your family and as a result, you find yourself alone. An air of darkness prevails, and you have lost sight of what is right and good in life. This is an unfortunate situation that will continue for an extended period. You can counteract the darkness of this time by being modest, even humble, and by inviting your friends, family, and associates to share in your abundance. Do not be so intent on being in control, but gently release your grip to allow others to have a say in making decisions. The pronouncement of this line is misfortune for the actions you have already taken.

56
LÜ

The Wanderer,
The Traveler

THE KUA

This kua depicts a traveler or wanderer whose stay is of short duration. Thus, only limited progress can be made. At this time, do not try to accomplish lofty goals or goals that require perseverance, for you or the person or situation at issue will not tarry long. If your question concerns your own situation, you are in a transitional state and will experience a change of some kind in the near future. If you are to make even the small progress possible under those changing conditions, you must conduct yourself with reserve, honor, and modesty. Refrain as well from forceful or aggressive behavior. Should any disputes arise, settle them quickly by meeting your adversary more than halfway, and be cautious when demanding restitution. Should you find yourself involved in a lawsuit, settle it quickly. Under no circumstances should you permit it to drag on, or you will suffer misfortune. If you travel to new places, be on your most courteous, cordial, best behavior, while avoiding all confrontation. Avoid arrogance as well.

During the time of traveling or wandering, do all the good you can so that, when you move on, those you have met or dealt with will speak well of you. If your question concerns a current situation, it will pass quickly and another situation will replace it.

The action you take regarding the current situation will shape the one that follows. If your question concerns a person, he or she will soon leave the situation. If your question concerns a condition or state of affairs, it will soon pass and evolve into a new condition. If you have obtained this as your second kua, the person, situation, or condition will move on, but not until some time has passed.

THE LINES

BOTTOM LINE: Because you are in the present situation or location for only a short time, you will obtain the best result possible if you avoid quibbling over petty items or issues. Remain focused on your main goal. Tolerate the mistakes of others and excuse even intentional violations. If you do not follow that guidance, you will incur misfortune.

LINE 2: You are in a place or situation where you have enough assets to maintain yourself, but you will soon move on. By behaving with dignity, generosity, kind-heartedness, and tolerance, you will find a loyal and trustworthy helper. Avoid arguments, conflicts, and pettiness. If you do find yourself involved in any type of conflict, resolve it as quickly as possible.

LINE 3: You have been overbearing, contentious, unforgiving, and inconsiderate. As a result, you will lose your lodging, your friends, and your helpers. If you have not already done so, read the section on "The Superior Person" (page 387). Study it and cultivate the qualities of character described there if you hope to avoid such consequences in the future. Your situation is now dangerous.

LINE 4: You have found a temporary place or situation and have the resources to sustain yourself, but your position is still unstable and requires that you be constantly on the alert for danger. Your best course of action is to be courteous, friendly, and sincere while maintaining a path of high ethical and moral values.

LINE 5: You are about to accomplish a worthy goal. Reaching your goal will bring you honor and a position of greater leadership. You will have the aid of those above and below you, and good fortune will be yours. If you find yourself traveling, you would do well to bring a gift to those you visit, for then you will find favor with them and will receive many benefits.

TOP LINE: Although you lose your position, you react by joking about it. Later on, however, you will grieve over the loss you have suffered. If you lose sight of the reality of your situation, which is that the topic under consideration is only temporary, and let yourself become immodest and intolerant, additional losses and misfortunes will befall you.

57
SUN

Gently Penetrating

THE KUA

The kua represents gentleness and ceaseless penetration into the consciousness of others so that you may influence them. It also represents the power of your mind to penetrate into the dark recesses where conspiracies and intrigues live, and to expose them to the light, where they can be dissolved. In addition, it represents your clarity of judgment, which allows you to reach decisions that will benefit you and protect you from being harmed by others' schemes or intrigues. The image is the gentle but ceaselessly penetrating wind. Because this kua is formed of the trigram Sun doubled, it means two winds, or wind following wind. The first wind penetrates into the situation and disperses negative or evil influences in the minds of those you wish to influence. The second wind penetrates into their consciousness and changes their attitudes so they will follow you willingly and help you to achieve your goals. You can help bring these changes about by repeating your orders or commands gently but consistently and by giving them a clear vision of your goal. If you try to use force, or if your manner is harsh or abrasive, you will fail to bring about the harmonious changes you are seeking, and their change in attitude will fade quickly.

Your goal is to create willingness and enthusiasm, not to bully those you wish to influence into reluctant or unwilling obedience. If you communicate your message gently, you will arouse neither resentment nor resistance. To do this, your message must be clear and grounded in ethical, moral intentions. It will be of great benefit if you are also patient and persevering. At this time, you will benefit by setting out to accomplish a goal of some kind. The ancient text suggests that you should seek the counsel of a qualified person before you begin, and as the work progresses. If you work for someone else or are working on someone else's behalf, you will do well to broadly communicate his or her wishes to others gently, but always consistently. Keep your goal in mind at all times. In this kua, success comes through taking small steps: achieving minor goals, paying attention to minor details, using minor players, and practicing modesty.

THE LINES

BOTTOM LINE: Your position is weak, and you lack strength and resources, but your indecisiveness is making matters worse. No one else is available or willing to help, so you must handle this situation on your own. If you wish to exert your influence, you must keep your goal firmly in your mind at all times, tell others what it is, and tell them what action you want them to take. Be decisive in your manner, and do not hesitate to repeat your orders as often as you need to, but do it gently so resistance does not arise. An obstacle of some kind is keeping you from reaching your goal. Use the penetrating force of your intellect to see to the core of this obstacle and to remove it. Gaining a complete understanding of this problem will require fierce determination and unceasing but gentle effort on your part.

LINE 2: Hidden, negative influences are affecting the situation. Turn to advisers who can help you to identify and deal with them; also, consulting the oracle can help you. You must identify and expose those negative influences, or they will continue to block your plans. You can and should get help from a person in a position of authority. Good fortune results without incurring blame.

LINE 3: You are putting off making important decisions. If you spend too much time debating your course of action, you will miss your opportunity. This is the time for taking action. Decide on your best course of action and move forward. Delay can cause you to miss what may be your only opportunity in this situation.

LINE 4: Your gentle, persistent efforts to reach your goal will result in an unusually successful conclusion, and you will be well rewarded for your efforts. Cooperation with those in authority will be smooth and advantageous. All causes for remorse disappear.

LINE 5: The beginning has not been good, but the time has come when a change can be implemented that will provide for a good ending. Change and improvement are what are now called for. Take great care in planning and carrying out your new plan. Once you begin, continue to monitor the situation carefully to make sure the change is being carried out properly. By proceeding in that manner, you will achieve good fortune.

TOP LINE: You have obtained an understanding of the dark forces that are at work in your situation, but because the forces are too powerful, you should not take further action to combat them at this time. There is an indication that you may have lost part of your assets, but do not retaliate because it will only cause further losses.

58
TUI

Joyousness, Pleasure

THE KUA

This kua is made up of the trigram for "Lake" doubled. Because the lake symbolizes joy, the kua represents lake feeding lake, or joy replenishing joy. The main difference between joy and pleasure is that joy comes from within, while pleasure comes from outside stimulation. Joy stems from powerful feelings of contentment and well-being, while pleasure stems from mental or physical sense gratifications. This kua shows that joy springs from inner strength and from following an honorable path, while pleasure, carried to extremes, can cause you harm.

If your question concerns a relationship, the indication is that the two of you will provide each other with joy. To maintain that joy, cultivate affection, consideration, and respect as the primary basis of your relationship. Focus your attention on having the relationship endure. Joy shared is joy doubled. The image of mutual joy leads to the idea of people gathering together to discuss the great truths of life and thereby expanding each other's ideas and conceptions about its wonder.

Success and good fortune lie ahead, so you should be joyous of heart but also serious-minded. Superior persons are always serious-minded at some level because they know that all periods of prosperity are followed by times of decline, and that all people are not as they should be. They therefore take thought for the future and exercise caution in their dealings with others. Nonetheless, no matter how serious or weighty their thoughts, those concerns never dim the inner joy they feel because of their continual awareness that they are indestructible children of the wonder-filled Universe of which they are an inseparable part. By following the guidance of this kua, you will meet with success.

THE LINES

BOTTOM LINE: You are at the beginning of joyousness. You possess the strength of will to avoid any excesses of pleasure that would ultimately detract from your joyousness, and you will therefore find within you a quiet contentment that will sustain you and heighten your joy. Because you desire little from without yet find happiness because of your philosophy, you are sure to meet with good fortune. You can sustain your joyous feelings by continuing to uphold high ethical and moral standards, walking the path of the superior person, and by being content with what you have.

LINE 2: A friend or associate will tempt you with inappropriate pleasures. Fortunately, you are strong enough to remain true to your high principles and sincere enough in your attitude to convey your refusal in a manner that will not offend your friend or associate. If you find yourself in the company of anyone who tempts you to stray from the path of utmost integrity, refuse courteously, and then stay away from that person. Both friendships and close relationships call for making choices. Some people uplift you, while others drag you down; some give you strength, while others sap your energy. So choose carefully.

Good friends, like good neighbors, are a lifelong blessing, but destructive relationships can ruin your entire life. If you continue to follow the path of the superior person, you will naturally and spontaneously seek out friends and associates who have admirable qualities and are of the highest integrity. By following the path of utmost integrity you will experience good fortune.

LINE 3: You are in a strong position, but there is a indication that you are finding it hard to resist pleasures that are inappropriate for you. Your wanting to indulge in such lowly pleasures comes from a feeling of emptiness. Instead, you should fill up the void with spiritual wisdom from which you can form a new philosophy that will keep you happy, and you will therefore require less from without. Avoid doing nothing, for it could put you in harm's way. Instead, involve yourself in a project that will occupy your mind, time, and energy, for, if you continue on your current pleasure-seeking path, you will suffer harm and misfortune.

LINE 4: You are strong but are being tempted by inappropriate pleasures. If you go on wavering between the desire to indulge in them or not indulge in them, you will not find the peace that leads to real joy. Joy will come only after you resolve your inner conflict in favor of steadfast commitment to the path of integrity. If you have not already done so, study the section on "The Superior Person" (page 387), and examine yourself to see if you are following that path of honor and high ethical standards. If you stray from it, you will suffer greatly, but if you commit yourself to the path of light and good, the ancient text states that you will find great joy.

LINE 5: You are strong and in a position of leadership. However, a person is tempting you to inappropriate pleasures that would bring you harm. To indulge this person by pretending to respect him or her and by acting as if you are even considering taking part in those low behaviors is degrading to you and can also lead to harmful consequences. You have the strength to resist that person, and you should do so.

TOP LINE: You have been unable to resist yielding to inappropriate pleasures. This can only have unfortunate consequences. If you continue along this path, you will suffer misfortune. The path of the inferior person, which always leads to misfortune, is directly in front of you. So is the path of the superior person, which always leads to good fortune. At every moment, you must choose between those two paths. Choose wisely, as you are creating your future with your decisions.

59
HUAN

Dissolve, Disintegrate, Dissipate, Unify

THE KUA

This indicates that a dangerous situation exists that you can resolve by identifying the danger and acting to gently dissolve or remove the dangerous elements. The source of the danger is disunity and a lack of harmony among those who should be unified and cooperating with you to achieve a common goal. If there is a lack of enthusiasm and dedication to a common goal, creating and maintaining unity will be difficult.

To obtain help in identifying the heart of the problem and in arriving at ways to remove the danger requires that you seek the guidance of the Universe in whatever way is appropriate for you, such as again inquiring of the oracle to obtain a deeper understanding of the problem. Speaking with the people involved will help you to learn what is keeping apart those who should be working together with you. If you make yourself a focal point, provide a common goal around which everyone can rally, and generate enthusiasm, as well as dissolving enmity, anger, hostility, and hatred, you will defeat the dangerous elements that are blocking unity. You can succeed in dissolving even the greatest danger, provided you persevere in searching for its source and in seeking ways to dissolve it. Success is certain.

THE LINES

BOTTOM LINE: This is the beginning of a dangerous situation. Here at the beginning, when unity and cooperation are essential, distrust and misunderstanding have taken over. You wish to join with someone or some group but because of the misunderstandings, you are finding it hard to make progress. It is up to you to identify and defeat whatever or whoever is standing in the way of unity. Fortunately, a powerful friend or associate will come forward to help you locate the source of the danger and to overcome it. If this friend is slow in appearing, ask for his or her help. You will have good fortune.

LINE 2: You are in the midst of a dangerous situation that is growing worse. Plans are falling apart, cooperation is disappearing, and discord is apparent. The source of the danger lies partially within you.

Either you have developed selfish motives, an attitude of uncooperativeness, egotistical desires, a distrust or dislike of your associates or friends, or you are harboring some hidden agenda that is at odds with the aims of your associates. You will continue to be in danger until you overcome your separatist tendencies and join with your friends or associates. If you proceed in that manner, you will achieve success. If you fail to find the source of the disunity, your difficulties will continue. During this time of conflict, maintain a positive and optimistic outlook, and avoid feelings of pettiness or hatred toward your friends and associates. You will have no regrets about having taken the appropriate action and no blame will attach to your actions.

LINE 3: You are nearing the end of a dangerous situation. It is so complex that it will take all your strength and energy to complete the task. You will have to set aside personal considerations until the danger is past and the goal is achieved. You will have no remorse for having acted in that manner.

LINE 4: At this time, you must sever your ties with a person or group to which you belong that is keeping you from achieving the more important goals that you set for yourself. That action will bring you supreme good fortune. It is easy to be swept away by outside influences, but if you are going to achieve your goal, you must be steadfast in your commitment to finish. By proceeding in that manner, no one will deter you from your chosen course. Your leaving will cause the group to dissolve, but another group will form, greater than the current one, of which you will be a part. This is an example of the law of "dispersing to accumulate," which is little known and seldom applied except by the wisest people.

LINE 5: You are strong and in a position of leadership. Despite the dangerous situation at present, in which disunity and conflict prevail, you will be inspired with a great idea that will unite your group. You will communicate it with such enthusiasm that everyone will follow your inspired leadership and thus end the conflict. Remain modest, and do not take credit. Instead, share it with others, and you will remain without blame for your actions.

TOP LINE: The situation has grown extremely dangerous. It is threatening you and possibly those close to you. You must identify whatever is causing the danger and take steps to immediately eliminate it. It is possible that you will have to keep a distance from whatever or whoever is the source of the danger. It is also your responsibility to keep those close to you safe from the danger.

60
CHIEH

Setting Limitations

THE KUA

The meaning of this kua is moderation. If life consisted of unlimited possibilities, it would only dissolve into the boundless. Just to consider every possibility would take all of eternity. Limitations are difficult to impose, particularly on yourself, but they are essential as well as effective. If you wish to truly enjoy the rewards of the life of a superior person, you must limit and regulate your activities, your thoughts, your associations, your relationships, your eating, your drinking, your sleeping, your work, your play, your accumulating, your spending—in fact, every aspect of your life. Everything in moderation benefits you; the same thing, carried to excess, will destroy you. Your goal is to set proper limits within which you will have total freedom. Because moderation in all things brings success, this kua also cautions you to moderate even your moderation, Do not impose such strict limitations that the limitations become excessive and damage you or others. You would also do well to set limits on your time and your tasks by dividing them into smaller segments so you can grasp and manage them more easily. It is essential that you define for yourself the kind of life you want to have and the best ways to achieve it, while using limitation to avoid excesses. Create a clear idea of the conduct you aspire to and the positive character traits you want to develop.

THE LINES

BOTTOM LINE: Here at the beginning of the situation, you have the strength and resources to move toward your goals, but you face obstacles too great to overcome. This is not a favorable time to move forward. Hold off and wait for a better time, which will soon come.

LINE 2: Favorable opportunities are at hand that require immediate action, but you are not taking action even though you have the strength, resources, and position to do so. If you fail to act now, you will miss your chance. That could lead to dangerous consequences and misfortune. Take immediate action to move toward your goal.

LINE 3: You have been self-indulgent, undisciplined, and given to excesses. To continue will expose you to danger and negative consequences. Stop immediately. Set manageable restraints and limits on your behavior. If you set limits on yourself now, you will avoid the danger and no one will find fault with you.

LINE 4: Impose limitations that are appropriate for you. If the limitations are too severe, negative consequences will result. Before attempting to impose limitations on your associates or subordinates, impose them on yourself. Proceeding in that manner, you will find that they will not react to your demands with resentment or resistance but with good natured compliance. As a result, both they and those in power will trust you, and you will rise to an even higher position of responsibility and success.

LINE 5: You are strong and have risen to a position of leadership. If you impose appropriate limitations on your own behavior, you will set a good example for those under you. If you then impose appropriate limitations on them, you will gain their cooperation and loyalty. Also, proceeding with your plans at this time will earn you both praise and approval. Good fortune lies ahead.

TOP LINE: The limitations and restrictions you have set for yourself or for others are too severe. If you persist, you risk unfortunate consequences. Easing the limitations will eliminate the possibility of future regrets and problems.

6 1
CHUNG FU

Emptiness, Openness

THE KUA

In this kua, two broken lines in the center of four solid lines represent emptiness. This is a time for you to be clear about your goals and about making decisions regarding others. The way in which you can achieve that clarity is by emptying your mind of all prejudiced thoughts, foregone conclusions, or conscious expectations. Let your mind be open, receptive, and free of preconceived ideas. Once you achieve that state of emptiness, you will be open to receiving wisdom and knowledge from other sources such as people, objects, books, and the Universe itself. It will be as if you have opened your pure mind—the mind you were born with—and are welcoming in infor- mation, knowledge, and wisdom. That openness will make it possible for you to perceive the state of mind of others. Your understanding of them will increase, and your ability to inspire them to follow you and to do your bidding will increase.

If you cultivate open-mindedness, you will earn the respect of all around you. You will also often find solutions that might otherwise escape you, and you will seldom make errors of judgment. Because you have opened your mind to vast sources of knowledge and information, you will speak words of such great wisdom that you will influence not only all those around you but also, as the ancient text states, "the pigs and fishes," which is a comical way of saying that you will influence even those who are hard to influence.

Practicing the pursuit of emptiness will bring you good fortune, and your perceptions will bloom like flowers during a perfect summer. Your inner clarity will make it possible for you to discuss difficult problems and to resolve them. You will benefit from undertaking a major project at this time, and it will bring you good fortune.

THE LINES

BOTTOM LINE: You are just at the beginning of this time of emptiness. Prepare yourself by pursuing openness and inner clarity. Eliminate prejudices, preconceived ideas, and fixed plans. Imagine that your mind is a pure receptive source, and that it welcomes information and knowledge, absorbs it, processes it, and makes excellent decisions based on it. See your mind as an empty blackboard on which the hand of the Universe will write. This preparation before beginning will bring good fortune. If you continue to hold to hidden motives or expectations in your mind while you try to achieve emptiness, you will fail in your attempt. If you prepare yourself properly, as described in this line and in the opening paragraph of this kua, you will have good fortune.

LINE 2: By achieving emptiness, you will influence people near and far by your words and deeds. You will attract those who share your goals, and they will come and also bring joy to the situation. Achieving emptiness is a result of your intention to welcome and be open to new information, to rid yourself of preconceived ideas, and to be fair and just in your decisions. Your most important goal should be to cultivate emptiness of mind, rather than consciously trying to produce an effect. Only then will you be receptive to the innermost thoughts of others and to the subtle promptings of the Universe.

LINE 3: You are depending on other people for your happiness and well-being. Sometimes that leads to happiness, and sometimes to sadness. If you depend on others for your happiness, you will be either happy or sad as your relationships rise and fall. To avoid such a fate, develop a quiet, self-contained joy, desiring nothing from without, and resting content with everything from within. You will then be able to remain independent and free because you harbor the quiet security of a heart fortified within itself.

LINE 4: You have almost achieved the emptiness that leads to insight, but outside influences have distracted you. Seek guidance from a wise person close to you, or from the leader, and you will find the right course again. If neither of those is available to you, seek emptiness on your own. In any case, no blame will attach to your progress.

LINE 5: You are strong and in a position of leadership. Because you have achieved openness and clarity, you can attract everyone you need to help you carry out your undertakings. They are attracted by your integrity and strength of character, and that is as it should be. No blame will attach to your progress.

TOP LINE: You are relying on words alone to influence your friends, associates, and others. At times, words alone may be effective, but this is not one of those times. To continue with words alone will bring misfortune. Your words are good, but it is through your actions and deeds that you will gain the confidence of others and influence them.

62
HSIAO KUO

Attention to Detail and Small Tasks, Avoiding Excesses

THE KUA

At this time, success lies not in reaching for lofty goals but in being content with small achievements meticulously carried out. This is a time when great modesty and conscientiousness will be well rewarded. Great good fortune can now be yours if you pay strict attention to minor details, aim for lesser goals, and guard against any extremes of behavior. In your spending, be thrifty, but avoid being stingy; if you lose someone in death, or learn of someone's great misfortune, grieve sincerely but avoid outward displays meant to impress others; in your conduct, be modest and avoid flattering others. In this time of attention to detail, an accumulation of many small goals will result in your achieving a major goal.

THE LINES

BOTTOM LINE: At this time of beginning, choose only extremely modest goals, and pay great attention to details. Any attempt to accomplish lofty goals will fail at this time. The ancient text states, "The bird meets with misfortune through flying." That means that, although the bird should stay in its nest, it does not; it flies away, and the hunter shoots it. The current situation presents some danger to you, but only if you try to accomplish a major goal. Do not stray from socially accepted courses of action or take any extreme steps. Practice modesty and caution, while all the time achieving small goals.

LINE 2: You will benefit from bypassing your subordinates and going directly to the leader or to those in authority to accomplish your goal. If you are rebuffed, make a connection with a lower-ranking member of the group, and carry out your assigned tasks. In no case should you expend great effort or expect tremendous results now. Behave modestly, and avoid trying to force an improvement in your rank or position. Instead, focus on fulfilling the duties of your present position with great care. If you proceed in that manner, no one will be able to direct any criticism at you.

LINE 3: You are acting overconfident, given the dangers of the present situation. If you do not use extreme caution, you may lay yourself open to misfortune from an unexpected quarter. The ancient text states, "Somebody may come up from behind and strike you." That saying is a metaphor for an unexpected attack. Therefore, pay great attention to details and leave nothing undone. This is a time when you must proceed with the utmost caution. Every step you take should be well thought out and highly organized. If you plunge ahead, thinking that you are invincible, you will find yourself in great difficulty.

LINE 4: You are strong and would like to advance, but to try to move forward will expose you to great danger. Do not attempt anything now. Instead, remain inwardly persevering, while outwardly keeping still. You may have a chance to meet with the leader or with someone in authority. Be extremely cautious and careful of what you say and do, and no blame will attach to you.

LINE 5: You are in the position of leadership, but lack the strength and resources to reach your goals. There are people around who can help you, but you must seek them out and enlist their aid. They are not prominent leaders but people in modest positions who have made outstanding accomplishments. It is by their accomplishments that you will be able to recognize them. With the aid of those helpers, exceptional tasks can be carried out in spite of all difficulties.

If you are uncertain if someone can help you or not, inquire of the oracle to find the answer.

TOP LINE: You have attempted or are attempting what is impossible for you to accomplish. In a time when only limited accomplishments are possible, your arrogant pursuit of unrealistic goals will bring failure and misfortune. Be content with what you have achieved and work toward extremely modest goals.

63
CHI CHI

Completion, In Place, in Order

THE KUA

This is the only kua in the I Ching in which all the lines are in their proper places: strong lines are in strong places, and weak lines are in weak places. Perfect order has been accomplished, inner and outer harmony prevail, and perfect position and balance have been achieved. That is the condition surrounding your question. Your future looks bright and prosperous. However, it is only after perfect balance has been achieved that any misstep brings imbalance.

The ancient text states, "No plain not followed by a slope, no increase not followed by a decrease." It is an eternal law of the Universe that everything turns toward its opposite as soon as it reaches its maximum potential: fullness to emptiness, light to dark, abundance to lack. Knowing that law, superior persons make provisions for a time of decrease in times of prosperity. In times of good health, they build themselves up, and so prepare against a time of illness. In times of safety, they take precautions that protect them in times of danger. They think ahead, so they are always prepared. They therefore enjoy a lifetime of good fortune and success.

This kua cautions you to pay close attention to details and to remain modest and alert now that you have acquired your treasure, whatever it is. Otherwise, the same law that brought it to you will take it away or will cause it to work against you.

Superior persons remain aware of the danger and do all they can to continue the order and balance as long as possible. You can prolong this time of perfect order by being vigilant and persevering and by paying attention to finishing the final details of your plan or situation.

THE LINES

BOTTOM LINE: Now that everything is in perfect order, there is a great pressing forward toward the accomplishment of major goals. You must be clear-sighted enough to see that forceful or aggressive action is dangerous and will lead to failure. Stop any such behavior immediately, and no blame will attach to your actions because of their correctness. Even so, you cannot completely escape the negative consequences of the actions already taken.

LINE 2: A small setback or loss will occur that prevents forward movement. Do not try to overcome the setback, for it will right itself, and any losses incurred will be recouped. During the time of waiting, you should be seeking to improve yourself so that when the time of waiting ends, you will be prepared to move forward.

LINE 3: Now that complete order has been achieved, you feel a strong urge to expand the scale of what you are trying to accomplish. That is possible, but it will mean a long, difficult, and exhausting struggle. If you move forward, be sure not to depend on or use inferior people. Think carefully about whether you want to take on a project that will require such enormous effort. You will be successful, but at a great cost to yourself. Wise people know what is enough. They do not overspend themselves, overreach themselves, or strive needlessly.

LINE 4: You have achieved a high position, close to the leader, and you communicate well with that person. You also have the support of your subordinates, and, in this time of perfect order, all seems to be well. However, danger lurks, and continuous caution is necessary if order is not to degenerate into disorder and your position close to the leader is not to work against you. Continue seeking ways to maintain this time of perfect balance and position. You can prolong your success by following a path of utmost integrity.

LINE 5: Here in this time of perfect order and harmony, you have reached the peak of leadership. Your success may cause you to want to offer elaborate celebrations and expensive gifts to those around you. However, such elaborate displays lack real warmth and feeling, and those around you will not receive them as well as they would smaller offerings given with simplicity and real sincerity. This is a time when you must pay extra attention to maintaining your success because it is at its peak. Remember how you achieved your success, and follow the same principles to maintain it.

TOP LINE: Whether by seeming accident or because of great perseverance, you have overcome a danger. Move on. Do not tarry in its aftermath, or it will trap you.

64
WEI CHI

In Order, Out of Place

THE KUA

You have almost achieved success. The lines of this kua, each of which represents your current condition, are in order because the broken and solid lines follow each other as they are supposed to. However, all of the lines are in spaces that are inappropriate for them; the broken lines are in strong spaces, and the solid lines are in weak places. The same is true for your own situation: everything is in order, but out of place. Whatever is out of place, whether it be a person, a group, a system, an object, or a process, is complete in every detail and is on the verge of success, but it is not performing the function for which it was intended or else is not in the correct position. Something is wrong with the situation. Therefore, it functions, but not efficiently or at its full potential. Fortunately, it is only one step away from its proper place or its proper use. That means that complete success is close, but so is danger, because further misplacement will result if extreme caution and good judgment are not exercised. The ancient text uses the example of a fox stepping on stones to cross a wide stream. After nearly completing his crossing, he slips, and his tail falls into the water. You, too, should be extremely cautious as you near your goal. Move toward the accomplishment of your goal cautiously but with confidence because the pronouncement of this kua is success.

THE LINES

BOTTOM LINE: You would like to bring the disorder to order as rapidly as possible, but the time for it is not right. Your best course of action at this time is to hold back and wait for a more favorable time. If you push forward now, you will fail in your efforts and be humiliated.

LINE 2: You have enough power, resources, and position to bring about the correct placement or correct functioning, but the time for it is not right. To try to bring order now will lead to failure. Bide your time, and, while you wait, strengthen your mind and body, consolidate your position, check your resources and your alliances, and prepare to move forward at the appropriate time, which will soon come. That way, when the time for action comes, you will be performing at optimum levels and will be able to move forward confidently. To persevere in that course of action brings good fortune.

LINE 3: You see the opportunity to make the transition into the proper position by moving aggressively forward against those who are preventing you from reaching your goal, but you lack the power to do so. Do not attempt to force progress on your own, or you will bring on misfortune. Instead, look for able helpers who can assist you in bringing about the necessary change. In that way you and your helpers will bring order out of confusion and create success.

LINE 4: The time has come to bring order to the situation. You have the strength and resources, as well as enough support from those above and below, to reach your goals. Even though the necessary transition will be long and difficult, you must and will overcome whatever stands in your way. If you persevere in an appropriate course of action and continue your effort until the transition is completed, you will attain honor and good fortune. The ancient text says, "For three years, great realms are awarded." That means that you will receive abundant rewards for your efforts, and that they will continue to come to you for an extended period of time.

LINE 5: This is the time of transition into the perfect order and position you have been waiting and working for.

Everything is in place for you to succeed. You have enough intelligence, insight, authority, and support to bring about the correct positioning. Use your influence to produce the necessary changes, and good fortune and success will accompany your actions. Your light will shine forth and make its influence felt so that the people can rally around you and your cause. The power of your own personality will be a guiding light which all will follow. The success you achieve will justify the means you use to achieve it, provided that you follow a path of utmost integrity. You will have good fortune.

TOP LINE: The transition is almost complete. You stand at the brink of success. Because everything is about to fall into perfect place and in the correct order, you and your associates want to celebrate. As long as you do not celebrate to excess, all will be well. Carrying your celebration to extremes will turn your success into failure.

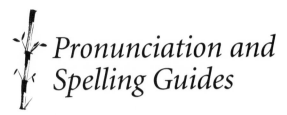

Pronunciation and Spelling Guides

The following guides list the sixty-four kua and the eight trigrams with the two main ways of spelling them in English and a guide to pronouncing each one.

Because the Chinese language does not have an alphabet, several systems for writing and recreating the sounds of Chinese words using the English alphabet have developed over time. The Wade-Giles system dates back to the mid-1800s, and many books about the I Ching still use its spellings. Out of respect for that tradition, I use it in this book. The Pinyin spelling system is the official system of the People's Republic of China—adopted about twenty-five years ago. Some students of the I Ching are now using its spellings instead of Wade-Giles, so you may find this list helpful if you pursue your studies of the I Ching. Each system has accuracies and inaccuracies in terms of how self-evident the pronunciations are. In some instances, there is no spelling difference between the two systems.

The pronunciation guide is my best attempt to capture the authentic sound of the kua and trigrams as they are spoken in standard Mandarin Chinese today.

WADE-GILES AND
PINYIN HEXAGRAMS

Kua Number	Wade-Giles Spelling	Pinyin Spelling	Pronunciation*
1	Ch'ien	Qian	chee • en
2	K'un	Kun	k'n
3	Chun	Zhun	juhn
4	Mêng	Meng	mung
5	Hsü	Xü	ssyu
6	Sung	Song	soong
7	Shih	Shi	shh
8	Pi	Bi	bee
9	Hsiao Ch'u	Xiao Xü	ss • ee • ow choo
10	Lü	Lü	lyu'
11	T'ai	Tai	tie
12	P'i	Pi	bee
13	T'ung Jên	Tong Ren	tohng rhen
14	Ta Yu	Da You	dah yoe
15	Ch'ien	Qian	chee • en
16	Yü	Yü	yu
17	Sui	Sui	sway
18	Ku	Gu	goo
19	Lin	Lin	lin
20	Kuan	Guan	gwahn
21	Shih Ho	Shi He	shh h'

*An apostrophe indicates almost no vowel sound.

Kua Number	Wade-Giles Spelling	Pinyin Spelling	Pronunciation
22	Pi	Bi	bee
23	Po	Bo	bo
24	Fu	Fu	foo
25	Wu Wang	Wu Wang	woo wahng
26	Ta C'hu	Da Xü	da ssyu
27	I	Yi	ee
28	Ta Kuo	Da Guo	da gwo
29	K'an	Kan	kahn
30	Li	Li	lee
31	Hsien	Xian	ssee • en
32	Hêng	Heng	h'ng
33	Tun	Dun	doon
34	Ta Chuang	Da Zhuang	dah djwahng
35	Chin	Jing	djeeng
36	Ming I	Ming Yi	meeng yee
37	Chia Jên	Jia Ren	djee • ah rhen
38	K'uei	Kui	kway
39	Chien	Jian	djee • en
40	Hsieh	Jie	dji• yeh
41	Sun	Sun	soon
42	I	Yi	ee
43	Kuai	Guai	gwy

Continued

Kua Number	Wade-Giles Spelling	Pinyin Spelling	Pronunciation
44	Kou	Gou	go
45	Ts'ui	Cui	tsway
46	Shêng	Sheng	shung
47	K'un	Kun	k'n
48	Ching	Jing	djing
49	Ko	Ge	g'
50	Ting	Ding	ding
51	Chên	Zhen	djenn
52	Kên	Gen	g'n
53	Chien	Jian	dji • ann
54	Kuei Mei	Gui Mei	gway may
55	Fêng	Feng	f'ng
56	Lü	Lü	lyu'
57	Sun	Xun	ssoon
58	Tui	Dui	dway
59	Huan	Huan	hwahn
60	Chieh	Jie	dji • yeh
61	Chung Fu	Zhong Fu	djong foo
62	Hsiao Kuo	Xiao Guo	ssee • ow gwo
63	Chi Chi	Ji Ji	djee djee
64	Wei Chi	Wei Ji	way djee

WADE-GILES AND
PINYIN TRIGRAMS

Wade-Giles Spelling	Pinyin Spelling	Pronunciation*
Ch'ien	Qian	chee • en
K'un	Kun	k'n
Chên	Zhen	djenn
Sun	Sun	soon
K'an	Kan	kahn
Li	Li	lee
Kên	Gen	g'n
T'ui	Dui	dway

---

*An apostrophe indicates almost no vowel sound.

# The Superior Person

In *I Ching Wisdom,* Volume I, it is stated:

> *Every person*
> *must have something to follow,*
> *a lodestar.*

Wu Wei's comment:

Everyone needs something to bring out the best in himself and to provide direction for his development. By holding the image of the superior person in your mind as your lodestar, you will achieve not only supreme success but also great happiness.

A few qualities of the superior person:

He is humble.

He is willing to let others go ahead of him.

He is courteous.

His good manners stem from his humility and concern for others.

He is good-natured.

He is calm.

He is always inwardly acknowledging the wonder he feels for all of creation.

He is willing to give another the credit.

He speaks well of everyone, ill of no one.

He believes in himself and in others.

He does not swear.

He is physically fit.

He does not overindulge.

He knows what is enough.

He can cheerfully do without.

He is willing to look within himself to find the error.

He is true to what he believes.

He is gentle.

He is able to make decisions and to act on them.

He is reverent.

He carries on his teaching activity.

He does not criticize or find fault.

He is willing to take blame.

He does not have to prove anything.

He is content within himself.

He is dependable.

He is aware of danger.

He is certain of his right to be here.

He is certain of your right to be here.

He is aware that the Universe is unfolding as it should.

He is generally happy.

He laughs easily.

He can cry.

It is all right with him if another wins.

His happiness for another's happiness is sincere.

His sorrow for another's sorrow is sincere.

He has no hidden agendas.

He is thrifty and therefore is not in want.

He finds a use for everything.

He honors everyone and is therefore honored.

He pays attention to detail.

He is conscientious.

He values everyone, and therefore everyone values him.

He is optimistic

He is trustworthy.

He is good at salvage.

He is patient.

He knows the value of silence.

He is peaceful.

He is generous.

He is considerate.

He is fair.

He is courageous in the face of fear.

He is clean.

He is tidy.

He does not shirk his duties.

He causes others to feel special.

He expects things to turn out well.

He is always seeking to benefit others in some way.

His presence has a calming effect.

He is not attached to things.

He sees obstruction as opportunity.

He sees opposition as a signpost deflecting him in the right direction.

He sets a good example.

He is joyous of heart.

He takes thought for the future.

He wastes nothing, and therefore he always has enough.

He has good manners.

He obtains nothing by force.

He overlooks the mistakes of others.

He has greatness of spirit.

He is clear-headed.

He does more than his share.

He meets others more than halfway.

He rests when it is time to rest; he acts when it is time to act.

He feels no bitterness.

He is forgiving.

He does not pretend.

He is not cynical.

He studies.

He reveres the ancient masters.

He is inspiring.

He nourishes nature and therefore is nourished by nature.

He leaves things better than he found them.

He does not make a show.

He practices goodness.

He is simple.

His intentions are always beneficial.

He is a wellspring of determination.

He does not boast.

He produces long-lasting effects.

He has endurance.

He is flexible in his thinking.

He does not overreach himself.

He does not overspend himself.

He does not strive foolishly.

He is consistent.

He does not go into debt.

He lives a simple life.

He nurtures his good qualities and virtues.

He is sensitive to his inner prompting.

He exists in the present.

He feels no break with time.

He is cautious.

He is kind.

He holds his goals lightly in his mind, allows no opposing thoughts to enter, and, as a result of natural law, is drawn inexorably to his goals.

He seeks enlightenment.

He sets limitations for himself within which he experiences complete freedom.

He is careful of his words, knowing that he is reflected in them.

He does not use flattery.

He depends on himself for his happiness.

He feels secure.

He knows the truth of his existence.

He does not strive for wealth, fame, popularity, or possessions.

He does not complain.

He turns back immediately having discovered that he has strayed from the path of the superior person.

He practices daily self-renewal of his character.

In *I Ching Wisdom,* Volume I, it is stated:

Only
through daily self-renewal of character
can you continue
at the height of your powers.

Wu Wei's comment:

It takes herculean effort to reach the peak of perfection in any area of life and continuous effort to remain there. Every day some effort should be expended in refreshing yourself with the ways of the superior person. Reading the *I Ching* or other great books, talking to like-minded people, teaching others, studying the deeds of our ancient heroes, thinking about your actions of the day to see whether you are being the best you can be; all are ways to successfully continue on the path. As you grow in awareness, your power grows, and your attainments will be like the harvest after a perfect summer. There is no other activity that rewards you as richly as the daily self-renewing of your character.

Final Guidance

Remember that every ending heralds a new beginning. No matter how poor your circumstances or how inadequate your personal situation, the path of the superior person, which leads only to supreme good fortune and great success, is always open to you. You may take the first step upon it at any time and thus, magically, transform your circumstances. Those benefits are available to everyone, withheld from no one, for the eternal, conscious, aware Universe, of which you are an inseparable part, wants you to succeed. On the other hand, the path of the inferior person is also always open to you, but only so that its lessons of hardship, misery, and despair will ultimately bring you to the truth. At each step of your way, you will have to choose between those two paths. Choose well, for your future is entirely in your own hands.

Wu Wei

Index

Key to Identifying the Kua

Upper→ Lower ↓	Ch'ien ☰	Chên ☳	K'an ☵	Kên ☶	K'un ☷	Sun ☴	Li ☲	Tui ☱
Ch'ien ☰	p. 75 **1**	p. 231 **34**	p. 97 **5**	p. 193 **26**	p. 121 **11**	p. 113 **9**	p. 137 **14**	p. 277 **43**
Chên ☳	p. 189 **25**	p. 321 **51**	p. 87 **3**	p. 197 **27**	p. 183 **24**	p. 271 **42**	p. 177 **21**	p. 155 **17**
K'an ☵	p. 101 **6**	p. 261 **40**	p. 205 **29**	p. 91 **4**	p. 105 **7**	p. 357 **59**	p. 377 **64**	p. 301 **47**
Kên ☶	p. 227 **33**	p. 369 **62**	p. 255 **39**	p. 325 **52**	p. 141 **15**	p. 329 **53**	p. 343 **56**	p. 215 **31**
K'un ☷	p. 127 **12**	p. 147 **16**	p. 109 **8**	p. 179 **23**	p. 81 **2**	p. 167 **20**	p. 235 **35**	p. 289 **45**
Sun ☴	p. 283 **44**	p. 221 **32**	p. 305 **48**	p. 157 **18**	p. 295 **46**	p. 347 **57**	p. 315 **50**	p. 201 **28**
Li ☲	p. 133 **13**	p. 339 **55**	p. 373 **63**	p. 175 **22**	p. 239 **36**	p. 245 **37**	p. 209 **30**	p. 309 **49**
Tui ☱	p. 117 **10**	p. 335 **54**	p. 361 **60**	p. 265 **41**	p. 163 **19**	p. 365 **61**	p. 251 **38**	p. 351 **58**